'REALLY HELF BUTTERFLIES

CW01501261

PRINTED EDITION, BOB FLOWERDEW 2018

Plants and Lepidoptera; the caterpillars and thus butterflies these plants support

-being Volume 2 of 'Plant Companions and Co-lives'

If we want more butterflies in our gardens we must provide exactly those suitable plants that can feed their respective larvae, caterpillars, grubs, worms and miners, and not just plant a few pretty flowers to attract the adults.

Also available:

'REALLY HELP YOUR PLANTS'

Plants and other plants, their good and bad companions and worst weeds

-being Volume 1 of 'Plant Companions and Co-lives'

'REALLY HELP YOUR GARDEN ECOLOGY'

Plants and their co-lives, their associated fauna, insects (other than Lepidoptera), nematodes, bacteria, fungi large & small and viruses

-being Volume 3 'Plant Companions and Co-lives'

'REALLY HELP YOUR CROPS'

Worst weeds, Companion plants and Co-lives,

for farmers and horticulturists

-specifically extracted data from vols.1-3

Dedication- to Joe Thompson without who's assistance I would never have got this done (and if you need a website or help with an ebook is contactable via my website.)

CONTENTS

Introduction

Key to text

A-Z Plants with which Lepidoptera larvae they sustain

Glossary, English common names and Latin to find them under.

INTRODUCTION

There are many books and sources recommending various flowers to 'feed the butterflies' and 'bring more butterflies to your garden'. However most fail on one major point- you cannot have a butterfly on a flower without its larva first eating the foliage of that or another plant! Providing a few more nectar sources does indeed feed the butterflies, but really does not increase their numbers or diversity. In fact you are just drawing them from elsewhere.

If we really want more butterflies in all our gardens we must also provide exactly those suitable plants that can feed their respective larvae, caterpillars, grubs, worms and miners.

Most larvae have a range of possible food plants and some eat almost anything. We do not need alter our gardens by much to help these especially the latter and if we grow any of their favourite plants we will almost certainly increase their numbers.

However some larvae are very particular and will not eat the wrong species let alone a different genus. To increase such butterflies and moths then we must cultivate exactly the 'correct' plants to feed their larvae. Naturally these must invariably be native plants, either as in the wild, or the garden forms of these.

If we increase the numbers of these plants then there is opportunity for these endangered insects to resurge.

Now misguidedly we gardeners have been recommending others not to plant double-flowered or similar blooms as 'these are destitute of nectar and or pollen and do not help wildlife'. However most often it's the foliage the caterpillar consumes so food-less flowers are less of a problem. With plants selected for flowering quite commonly the leaves still closely resemble the wild form. Thus garden flowers derived from native species will usually be as suitable as the wild form and should be chosen in preference to non-native plants. However, although a hybridised or 'imported' garden species of the same genus is not exactly the same plant as the native it may yet feed some larvae as there is the possibility of drift to these where the exact plant is unavailable.

Concentrating on the most endangered

Many, about 200 by current estimate, of our butterflies and moths have caterpillars that can only survive by eating one particular variety of native plant. So when but one species of a genus is thought to be the Sole sustainer of a particular caterpillar this is vitally important to know and important to grow. (In a few cases where two sustaining plants are very similar and both scarce species of the same scarce genus these have been counted as one.)

Unfortunately if that particular plant sustainer is not already growing nearby then the associated insect is also unlikely to be present locally so growing the sustainer may seem pointless. However we might grow some just in case such a highly dependent insect does pass by. After all butterflies can be blown far from home, some even across the Atlantic every so often.

When a plant is thought to be <u>One of two sustainers</u> of a larva then increasing numbers of one and / or both these plants is potentially highly beneficial for that butterfly and again more likely to be successful when one or other sustainer is already found locally. (Again very scarce similar species counted as one.)

Likewise plants thought to be <u>One of three sustainers</u> are still feeding larvae much at risk, particularly when as too often most of these sustainers are becoming scarce.

The plant is noted to 'Sustain' a given larva where more than three alternative plants are known to feed the larva. This situation is less critical to an insects survival as with more than three there is a much greater chance of at least one of them being found locally.

However the reduction of 'wild' places and our obsession with 'tidying-up' areas means many once common native plants are now scarce and need cultivating. For these are the very same plants that sustain the greatest variety of different larvae. Simply growing more of these potentially aids the most.

If you want to know whether a plant is local then look it up in your areas 'Flora', in the UK there is at least one for each county and most are very detailed.

What larvae eat

Most larvae cause damage to the plant by eating foliage thus reducing leaf area, however this is damage healthy plants can endure (as light passes through 'holes' and is then collected by lower leaves previously shaded) and often recover from. For example oaks spontaneously generate fresh or Lammas growth in summer to augment the older worn and more bothered foliage.

Some larvae can only digest younger foliage as older leaves become toxic or too tough, so these can eat a specific plant only during Spring or in times of new growth. To aid these cut back a few plants in a clump on a cycle so young foliage is available over a longer period. (As so many of the best sustainers are native trees which are highly desirable but do not suit modern gardens then these can be planted and annually coppiced, that is cut to the ground in winter, this will keep them relatively compact while still useful to the majority of suitable larvae.)

Some, mostly over-wintering, larvae want to consume different sustainers before and after hibernation thus requiring both plants to be present and relatively close to each other, and also near a potential safe hibernation site.

Sometimes other parts are also or solely eaten this causing worse or less damage than a simple reduction in leaf area. If the larvae usually or predominantly consumes other parts as well or instead of the foliage this is noted after the name thus (eats flowers), (seeds), (stems) and (roots).

In those cases where a larva is known to mostly consume other co-lifes or associates of the plant such as (dead leaves), (lichens) or (algae), this is also noted.

Some larvae are just so damn greedy, and prolific, they seriously damage the plants so these are then said to 'Suffer' rather than Sustain them. And marginal examples where the court is still out are said to 'Sustain / suffer' these.

On flowers

Although there is less need for more flowers for the adults than there is for more suitable foliage for the larvae we should still try to ensure there are plenty, and particularly of the scarcer natives.

Most butterflies and moths have a remarkably long proboscis with which they imbibe nectar. This can reach down into tubular flowers or pick at the shallow nectaries of massed tiny blooms, meaning they're able to feed on almost any flower with nectar. Most tubular shaped flowers have deep nectaries and are designed for butterflies and moths and to exclude other insects, whereas shallow and open mouthed nectaries are more suited for bees and flies but cannot stop butterflies supping too.

Though some Lepidoptera are exclusively particular, most have preferences but the majority are not too concerned about which flower they dine on. Some can be quite promiscuous, going wherever they can take a meal, even supping from other wet articles in the environment including manures and decaying fruits. The plants known to be heavy nectar producers are noted.

In general blue flowers appeal to bees, it's the yellow, orange and red flowers that appeal to butterflies and pale, violet or white blooms, especially night scented ones, which particularly attract moths who can find them from many miles distant.

As both butterflies and moths use their sense of smell we find scented flowers are often as attractive for them as well as a pleasure to us. Indeed where a particular flower is visited by a particular butterfly or moth this may itself smell similar- the flowers are mimicking a mate!

ON SIZE-ISM
To some only the largest most garish butterflies will please, small drab ones and most moths sadly do not. Yet all are curious, have their place in the scheme of things, and a diminutive

appearance may delight your close attention with a hand lens or camera app.

CATERPILLARS / MAGGOTS / GRUBS / 'WORMS' (NOT EARTHWORMS) / MINERS

If you want the butterflies someone somewhere's got to have the caterpillars, maggots, grubs, miners or 'worms'.

Many wriggling things are some form of Lepidoptera larvae (or larvae of flies, sawflies, beetle grubs and other groups, these will be found in volume 3). Anyway all are doing much the same thing to plants; that is bits go missing. As mentioned above whereas we generally think of larvae as leaf eaters some consume the insides of stems, flowers, seeds, capsules and storage organs instead of the foliage, or as well. So most larvae are quite undoubtedly not very plant friendly.

However only a few are so voracious and in such numbers they hazard a plants very existence if only from their own self interest. Yet these may threaten our own harvest or crop, so with these ecological co-lives, so called 'pests', then more detail is included.

Where six or more different larva may consume the foliage of each particular plant the total number sustained and or suffered is given at the start of that entry. There is necessarily repetition where multiple species support a similar range of larvae so for a few entries such as Quercus, Rumex and Salix those co-lives sustained by almost all species are listed under the initial genus heading.

WHAT TO DO NOW

We simply need grow a wider diversity of plants to feed more different caterpillars. The most suitable plants are invariably natives however these can be selected and improved forms with 'better' flowers. Dwarf more compact forms may probably be as useful as the originals. Likewise very similar very closely related though non-native species and varieties may prove viable. However most pretty 'aliens' may have useful flowers but seldom feed native larvae. I leave it to you to choose.

KEY

to text on the naming of plants and co-lives

Plant A-Z entries are alphabetical in Latin, in bold eg. **Acer** followed by species under discussion eg. campestre, then common name(s) in capitals eg. FIELD MAPLE. Thus **Acer** campestre, FIELD MAPLE.

Where A-Z entries are not plants but are important or generic terms, these are entered in plain capitals eg. ALGAE.

Lepidoptera co-lives are referred to by their English common name and to prevent confusion the Latin follows, but without the intervening comma as used with plant names eg. Green-veined White Pieris napi, and Orange-Tip Anthocaris cardamines.

Where alternative common and Latin names are derived from old reference books, and recognised as such, these are entered spaced with / as in **Galium** aparine, GOOSE-GRASS / CLEAVERS and Willow Beauty Alcis rhomboidaria / gemmaria.

Common names of other plants and co-lives embedded in the text are entered without initial capitals unless important to the case in question. Where necessary for clarity Latin names are employed and always started with a capital.

Some serious confusion occurs as Latin names keep being changed, this adding a huge level of complexity. Thus after the most recent still commonly accepted name may follow a string of older or newer genus and species names. My profuse apologies for the inelegant, indigestible chain this has created in places.

Although great effort has been made to determine the exact species and variety under discussion many notes have necessarily been gleaned from old literature where a then-common common-name was used. So occasionally there will be 'wrong' identifications. Most probably this will be the substitution of a widespread species or variety in place of an originally local one employing the same or similar (eg. references to 'Chamomile' have often proved misnomer or misidentification).

Also bear in mind that although a particular genus and species may be noted as having a certain association there is a strong probability that other species in the same genus will have the same or similar associations which so far have gone unrecorded.

Please accept my apologies for any errors, and let me know so the next edition can be corrected.

A-Z

ABIES ALBA / PECTINATA AND OTHER SPECIES, FIR-TREES

Sustain 7 Lepidoptera larva, 4 on foliage and 3 on algae on bark and dead wood.

One of three sustainers of 3: Spruce Carpet Thera variata other sustainers being other Abies species and Pseudotsuga douglasii, Scarce Footman Eilema complana (on algae) other sustainers being algae on Prunus spinosa and Rubus species, and Orange Footman Eilema sororcula / aureola (on algae) other sustainers being algae on Pinus and Quercus species.

Also sustains: Bordered White Bupalus piniaria, Satin Beauty moth Deileptenia ribeata / abietaria, Willow Beauty Alcis rhomboidaria / gemmaria, and Red-necked Footman Atolmis rubricollis (on algae).

ACER CAMPESTRE, FIELD MAPLE

Sustains 13 Lepidoptera larva on foliage.

Sole sustainer of 3: Mocha Cosymbia annulata / omicronaria, Maple Pug Eupithecia interbata / subciliata, and Maple Prominent Lophopteryx cucullina / cuculla.

One of two sustainers Plumed Prominent Ptilophora plumigera other being Acer pseudo-platanus.

One of three sustainers of 2: Small Yellow Wave Hydrelia flammeolaria / luteata others being Alnus and Sorbus aucuparia, and Treble Brown-spot Sterrha trigeminata / scutularia (eats flowers) others being Betula and Hedera.

Also sustains: Coxcomb Prominent Lophopteryx capucina / camelina, Satellite Eupsilia transversa / satellitia, Barred Sallow Tiliacea aurago, Sycamore Apatele aceris, Nut-tree Tussock Colocasia coryli, and Mottled Pug Eupithecia exiguata.

ACER PSEUDO-PLATANUS, SYCAMORE

Sustains 7 Lepidoptera larva.

<u>One of two sustainers</u> Plumed Prominent Ptilophora plumigera other being Acer campestre above.

Also sustains: Northern Winter moth Operophtera fagata / boreata, Barred Sallow Tiliacea aurago, Sycamore Apatele aceris, Yellow-barred Brindle Acasis viretata (eats flowers first, then on green berries then leaves), Buff-Tip Phalera bucephala, and Copper Underwing Amphipyra pyramidea.

ACHILLEA MILLEFOLIUM, YARROW

Long flowering blooms observed visited by at least 87 different insect species: 6 butterflies and moths, 30 species bee, 21 species diptera flies and 30 others.

Sustains 14 Lepidoptera larva on foliage: Ruby Tiger Phragmatobia fuliginosa, Cinnabar Callimorpha jacobaea, Sussex Emerald Thalera fimbrialis, Wormwood Pug Eupithecia absinthiata / minutata, Bordered Pug Eupithecia succenturiata, Black-veined moth Siona lineata / dealbata, Straw Belle Aspitates gilvaria. Probably sustains Portland Ribbon Wave Sterrha degeneraria, and Mullein Wave Scopula marginepunctata / promutata / incanata, Tawny-speckled Pug

Eupithecia icterata / subfulvata (eats flowers, seeds and leaves), Lime-speck Pug Eupithecia centaureata / oblongata (mostly eats flowers), Ling Pug Eupithecia goossensiata / minutata (mostly eats flowers), and V Pug Chloroclystis coronata (mostly eats flowers).

Suffers serious attacks by Belted Beauty Nyssia zonaria.

Aconitum lycoctonum, WOLF'S-BANE

<u>Sole sustainer</u> of Pease Blossom Periphanes delphinii.

<u>One of two sustainers of 2:</u> Purple-shaded Gem Plusia variabilis / illustris other being Thalictrum, and Golden Plusia Polychrisia moneta (feeds on seed pod first) other sustainer being **A. anthora**.

Aconitum napellus, MONKSHOOD

<u>Sole sustainer</u> of Pease Blossom Periphanes delphinii.

Also sustains Golden Plusia Polychrisia moneta (on seed pod at first).

Actaea spicata, BANEBERRY

Sustains Fern moth Horisme tersata.

Aesculus hippocastanum, HORSE CHESTNUT

Sustains Sycamore Apatele aceris.

AGERATUMS

Said to contain substances toxic to caterpillars.

AGRIMONIA EUPATORIA, AGRIMONY

Sustains Grizzled Skipper Pyrgus malvae / alveolus.

AGROPYRON JUNCEUM, SAND QUITCH / SAND COUCH-GRASS

One of two sustainers Sandhill Rustic Luperina nickerlii /gueneei / incerta other being Lepturus.

Also sustains Coast Dart Euoxa cursoria.

AGROPYRON REPENS, COUCH / WITCH / TWITCH / QUACK GRASS ET AL.

Sustains 20 Lepidoptera larva.

One of two sustainers of 2: Beautiful Gothic Leucochlaena hispida / oditis other being Poa, and Marbled Minor Procus strigilis (inside stems) other being Dactylis.

One of three sustainers of 2: Essex Skipper Thymelicus lineola others being Brachypodium pinnatum and Phleum pratense, and Dark Arches Apamea monoglypha / polyodon others being Dactylis glomerata and Poa annua.

Also sustains: Dusky Brocade Apamea obscura / gemina / remissa, Speckled Wood / Wood Argus Pararge negeria, Wall butterfly Pararge megera, Grayling Satyrus semele, Hedge Brown / Gatekeeper Maniola tithonus, Meadow Brown Maniola jurtina, Ringlet Aphantopus hyperantus, Large Skipper Ochlodes venata

/ sylvanus, Drinker Philudoria potatoria, Lunar Yellow
Underwing Triphaena orbona / subsequa, Common Wainscot
Leucania pallens, White Point Leucania albipuncta, Orange
Wainscot / Brown-line Bright-eye Leucania conigera, Slender
Brindle Apamea scolopacina, Common Rustic Apamea secalis /
oculea / didyma (inside stems), and Dusky Sallow Eremobia
ochroleuca (on seeds).

AGROSTIS CANINA, BENT GRASS

Sustains Antler Cerapteryx graminis.

AIRA CAESPITOSA, TUFTED HAIR-GRASS

Sustains 16 Lepidoptera larva.

Sole sustainer of 2: Small Dotted Buff Petilampa minima (on root
crown), and Middle-Barred Minor Procus fasciuncula (inside
shoots).

One of two sustainers of 2: Anomalous Stilbia anomala other
sustainer being Poa annua, and Scotch Argus Erebia aethiops /
blandina / medea other being Molinia caerula.

One of three sustainers of 4: Cloaked Minor Procus furuncula /
bicoloria others being Arrhenatherum elatius, Festuca elatior,
Hedge Rustic Tholera cespitis others being Aira flexuosa and
Nardus stricta, and Clouded-Bordered Brindle Apamea crenata /
rurea others being Primula species.

Also sustains: Ringlet Aphantopus hyperantus, Antler Cerapteryx
graminis, Common Wainscot Leucania pallens, Deep Brown Dart
Aporophyla lutulenta, Black Rustic Aporophyla nigra, Grayling

Satyrus semele, Clouded Brindle Apamea characterea / hepatica, Confused Apammea furva, and Common Rustic Apamea secalis / oculea / didyma (inside stems).

Aira caryophyllea, SILVERY HAIR-GRASS

<u>One of three sustainers</u> Straw Underwing Thalpolphila matura / eytherea others being Nardus and Poa species.

Aira flexuosa, WAVY HAIR-GRASS

<u>One of three sustainers</u> Hedge Rustic Tholera cespitis others being Aira caespitosa and Nardus species.

Also sustains Large Heath / Marsh Ringlet Coenonympha tullia / davus / tiphon.

Aira praecox, EARLY HAIR-GRASS

Sustains Grayling Satyrus semele.

Alchemilla alpina, ALPINE LADY'S-MANTLE

Sustains: Red Carpet moth Xanthorhoe munitata, and Dark Marbled Carpet Dysstroma citrata / immanata (eats flowers).

Alchemilla vulgaris / mollis, COMMON LADY'S-MANTLE

Traps water in the leaves as droplets so available to insects.

Sustains: Red Carpet moth Xanthorhoe munitata, and Knotgrass moth Acronycta / Apatele rumicis.

ALGAE

Some of the most important plants usually going unnoticed, a tremendous source of food for other living organisms especially in wet and marine conditions. Destroyed by most herbicides their loss is not heeded until detrimental side effects appear. Lichens are symbiotic relationship of algae and fungi, neither can survive as well alone as together, a visible result of a common process that goes on in the soil all the time.

Sole sustainer of the Red-necked Footman Atolmis rubricollis is the green algae coating many trees especially their dead wood.

Sole sustainer of the Muslin Footman Nudaria mundana is the green algae and associated lichens found on rock, stone, tile, dead wood etc.

ALISMA PLANTAGO-AQUATICA, WATER PLANTAIN.

Sustains Gold Spot Plusia festucae.

ALLIARIA OFFICINALIS, GARLIC MUSTARD

Sustains / suffers Green-veined White Pieris napi, and Orange-Tip Anthocaris cardamine.

ALNUS GLUTINOSA, ALDER

Sustains 40 different Lepidoptera larva.

Sole sustainer of 2: Conformist Graptolitha furcifera / conformis, and Dingy Shell Euchoeca nebulata / obliterata / heparata.

One of two sustainers of 4: Alder Kitten Harpyia bicuspis other being Betula, Pebble Hook-Tip Drepana falcataria / falcula other being Betula, Kentish Glory Endromis versicolora other being Betula, and Grey Birch Aethalura punctulata other being Betula.

<u>One of three sustainers of 4</u>: Common Fanfoot Herminia barbalis others being Betula and Quercus species, Dingy Mocha / orbicularia others being Salix atrocinerea and Salix caprea, Small Yellow Wave Hydrelia flammeolaria / luteata others being Acer campestre and Sorbus aucuparia, Sharp-angled Peacock Semiothisa alternaria / alternata others being Prunus spinosa and Salix caprea.

Also sustains: Lime Hawkmoth Mimas tiliae, Lobster Moth Stauropus fagi, Iron Prominent Notodonta dromedaries, Coxcomb Prominent Lophopteryx capucina / camelina, Common Lutestring Tethea duplaris, December Moth Poecilo campapopuli, Common Quaker Orthosia stabilis, Dark Brocade Eumichtis adusta, Brown-Spot Pinion Anchocelis litura, Nut-tree Tussock Colocasia coryli, Large Emerald Geometra papilionaria, Coronet Craniophora ligustri, Miller Apatele leporine, Blue-bordered Carpet Plemyria bicolorata / rubiginata, Autumn Green Carpet Chloroclysta miata, May Highflyer Hydriomena coerulata / impluviata / trifasciata, Mottled Pug Eupithecia exiguata, Early Tooth-striped Nothopteryx carpinata / lobulata, Autumnal Moth Oporinia autumnata, Pale November Moth Oporinia christyi, Waved Carpet Hydrelia testaceata / sylvata, Common White Wave Cabera pusaria, Common Wave Cabera exanthemata, Canary-shouldered Thorn Deuteronomos alniaria / tiliaria, Bordered Beuaty Epione repandaria / apiciaria, Buff-Tip Phalera bucephala, Emperor Saturnia pavonia / carpini, and Hebrew Character Orthosia gothica, Swordgrass Xylena exsoleta.

Plus lichens on limbs sustain Dingy Footman Eilema griseola.

ALSINE / ARENARIA, SANDWORTS

<u>One of three sustainers</u> of Sharp-angled Carpet Euphyia unangulata others being Rubus idaeus and Stellaria.

Possibly sustains Bright Wave Sterrha ochrata / ochrearia.

ALTHAEA / ALCEA ROSEA, HOLLYHOCK,

<u>One of two sustainers</u> Mallow Larentia clavaria / cervinata other being Malva.

Also sustains / suffers Dot Melanchra persicariae.

Suffers Angle Shades moth Phogophora meticulosa (on leaves, flowerbuds and blooms).

ALYSSUM SAXATILE / AURINIA SAXATILIS)

Flowers rich in nectar.

Sustains / suffers: Bath White Pontia daplidice, and Gem moth Nycterosea obstipata / fluviata / gemmata.

AMELANCHIER SPECIES, SNOWY MESPILUS / JUNE BERRY / SHADS

Sustains Small Eggar Eriogaster lanestris.

AMPELOPSIS SPECIES

Climbers often confused with Parthenocissus and Vitis so sometimes called, erroneously, Virginia creeper.

Sustains Silver Striped Hawkmoth Hippotion celerio.

Anacamptis pyramidalis, PYRAMID ORCHID

UK native, floral scent of cloves by day attracts butterflies, oddly at night smells of foxes.

Anagallis arvensis, SCARLET PIMPERNEL

<u>One of three sustainers</u> Dwarf Cream Wave Sterrha fuscovenosa / interjectaria / dilutaria / osseata others being Polygonum arvense and Taraxacum, and possibly mosses.

Anemone

The garden species and hybrids sustain / suffer Angle Shades moth Phogophora meticulosa (on leaves, flowerbuds and blooms, especially of St Brigid anemones).

Anemone nemorosa, WOOD ANEMONE

Sustains Twin-spot Carpet Colostygia didymata, and Fern Horisme tersata.

Angelica sylvestris, WILD ANGELICA

<u>One of three sustainers</u> White-spotted Pug Eupithecia tripunctaria / albipunctata (mostly eats flowers) others being Heracleum and Pastinaca.

Also sustains: Swallow-tail Papilio machaon, Triple-spotted Pug Eupithecia trisignaria (eats flowers and seeds), and V Pug Chloroclystis coronata (eats flowers).

Antennaria dioica, MOUNTAIN EVERLASTING

One of two sustainers Scarce Marbled Eublemma noctualis / paula (eats flowers) other being Gnaphalium.

Anthemis arvensis, CORN CHAMOMILE

One of two sustainers Vestal Rhodometra sacraria the other being Polygonum aviculare (also on A. nobilis).

Also sustains: Gem moth Nycterosea obstipata / fluviata / gemmata, and Chamomile Shark Cucullia chamomillae (eats flowers).

Anthemis cotula, STINKING MAYWEED

Usefully warm up their flower heads to aid pollinators.

Sustains Chamomile Shark Cucullia chamomillae (eats flowers).

Anthemis nobilis, CHAMOMILE, ROMAN CHAMOMILE

Often confused with other similar plants so see also Matricaria and Chrysanthemum entries.

One of two sustainers Vestal Rhodometra sacraria other being Polygonum Aviculare (also on A. arvensis).

Also sustains: Bordered Pug Eupithecia succenturiata, and Chamomile Shark Cucullia chamomillae (eats flowers).

ANTHRISCUS CAUCALIS / CHAEROPHYLLUM ANTHRISCUS / BUR(R) CHERVIL,

One of two sustainers Chimney Sweeper Odezia atrata / chaerophyllata other being Conopodium (also on similar A. temulum).

One of three sustainers Single-dottted Wave Sterrha dimidiata / scutulata (eats flowers) others being Pimpinella and Galium.

ANTHRISCUS SYLVESTRIS / CHAEROPHYLLUM SYLVESTRE, WILD CHERVIL

Sustains Double-striped Pug Gymnoscelis pumilata (eats flowers).

ANTHRISCUS TEMULUM / CHAEROPHYLLUM TEMULUM, ROUGH CHERVIL

One of two sustainers Chimney Sweeper Odezia atrata / chaerophyllata other being Conopodium (also on A. caucalis).

Also sustains: Gold Spangle Plusia bractea (in spring), Plain Golden Y Plusia iota, Beautiful Golden Y Plusia pulchrina, and Twin-spot Carpet Colostygia didymata.

ANTHYLLIS VULNERARIA, KIDNEY VETCH

Sustains 6 Lepidoptera larva.

One of two sustainers Small Blue Cupido minimus / alsus other being Melilotus.

Also sustains: Chalkhill Blue Lysandra coridon, Mazarine Blue Cyaniris semiargus / acis, Grass Eggar Lasiocampa trifolii, Bloxworth Blue Everes argiades / tiresias (eats flowers), and Hoary Footman Eilema caniola (algae and lichens).

Antirrhinum majus, SNAPDRAGON

<u>One of two sustainers</u> Toadflax Pug Eupithecia linariata (in flowers) other being Linaria.

Also sustains: Striped Hawkmoth Celerio livornica, and suffers Angle Shades moth attacks.

ANTS

Inadvertantly sustain a pretty moth Myrmecozella ochracella whose larvae feed on nest material of Formica rufa and F. pratensis.

Another tiny moth, Brachmia gerronella, has often been found in Lasius fuliginosus nests.

Sustain the rare Large Blue Lycaena arion, the larvae feed on wild thyme then move into ant nests to complete their last stage protected, and possibly fed by the ants. There is a long standing worldwide observation that ants have a very special relationship with 'Blue' Lepidoptera caterpillars; over 60 different species in 29 genera of Lycaenidae are closely associated with ants. Many of these caterpillars have a gland on the eleventh ring that oozes 'nectar' which the ants consume and in return the ants keep away parasites such as Ichneumon wasps. This has been observed in Long-tailed Blue Lampides boeticus, Chalkhill Blue Agriades coridon, and the American Celastrina pseudargiolus (very similar to our Holly / Azure Blue Celastrina argiolus).

Apium graveolens, CELERY
Sustains Swallow-tail Papilio machaon.

Sustains damage to roots from Small / Garden Swift moth Hepialus lupulinus, which also attacks beans, parsnip, lettuce, potato, strawberry and grass roots.

Aquilegias, COLUMBINES
Sustains Grey Chi moth Antitype chi.

Arabis glabra, TOWER MUSTARD
Sustains Orange-Tip Anthocaris cardamines.

Arctium lappa / majus, BURDOCK
Sustains: Ghost / Otter Moth Hepialus lupuli, Setaceous Hebrew Character Amathes e-nigrum, Epiblema scutulana (in stems), and Frosted Orange Gortyna flavago / ochracea (in stems).

Arctium minus, LESSER BURDOCK
Sustains: Painted Lady Vanessa cardui, and Burnished Brass Plusia chrysitis.

Arctostaphylos uva-ursi, BEARBERRY
Sustains 8 Lepidoptera larva.

One of three sustainers of 3: Northern Dart Amathes alpicola / hyperborea / alpina others being Empetrum and Vaccinum myrtillus, Broad-bordered White Underwing Anarta melanopa others being Vaccinium myrtillus and Vaccinium vitis-idaea, and Netted Mountain-Moth Isturgia carbonaria others being Betula and Salix aurita.

Also sustains: Small Dark Yellow Underwing Anarta cordigera, Golden-rod Brindle Lithomoia solidaginis, Saxon Hyppa rectilinear, Green Hairstreak Callophrys rubi (eats blossoms and leaves), and Satyr Pug Eupithecia satyrata (eats flowers).

Arenaria / Alsine, SANDWORT
Sustains Bright Wave Sterrha ochrata / ochrearia.

Arenaria peploides, SEA SANDWORT / SEA CHICKWEED
Sustains: Coast Dart Euoxa cursoria, Archer's Dart Agrotis vestigialis / valligera, Bright Wave Sterrha ochrata / ochrearia, and Bordered Sallow Pyrrhia umbra / marginata (eats flowers and seeds).

Armeria maritime, THRIFT
Sustains 6 Lepidoptera larva.

Sole sustainer of Crescent Dart Agrotis trux / lunigera.

Also sustains: Ground Lackey Malacosoma castrensis, Feathered Ranunculus Eumichtis lichenea, Sweet-Gale Apatele euphorbiae / myricae, Black-Banded Antitype xanthomista / nigrocincta (eats flowers), and Annulet Gnophos obscurata / pullata (eats flowers).

ARMORACIA RUSTICANA, HORSERADISH

Sustains / suffers: Green-veined White Pieris napi, and Garden Carpet Xanthorhoe fluctuata.

ARRHENATHERUM ELATIUS, FALSE-OAT, OAT GRASS

One of three sustainers Cloaked Minor Procus furuncula / bicoloria (in stems) others being Aira caespitosa and Festuca elatior.

ARTEMESIA ABROTANUM, SOUTHERNWOOD

Sustains Scarce Wormwood Shark Cucullia artemisiae / abrotani (eats flowers), and Feathered Footman Coscinia striata / grammica (on seeds).

ARTEMESIA ABSINTHUM / PRINCEPS, WORMWOOD

Sustains 7 Lepidoptera larva.

One of three sustainers Angle-barred Pug Eupithecia innotata (flowers) others being other Artemesia species.

Also sustains: Sussex Emerald Thalera fimbrialis, Wormwood Pug Eupithecia absinthiata / minutata, Bordered Pug Eupithecia succenturiata, Wormwood Shark Cucullia absinthii (seeds and buds), Feathered Footman Coscinia striata / grammica (on seeds), and Scarce Wormwood Shark Cucullia artemisiae / abrotani (eats flowers).

ARTEMESIA CAMPESTRIS, FIELD SOUTHERNWOOD

Sole sustainer Spotted Clover Heliothis scutiosa (eats flowers).

One of three sustainers Angle-barred Pug Eupithecia innotata (eats flowers) others being other Artemesia species.

Also sustains: Feathered Footman Coscinia striata / grammica (on seeds), and Scarce Wormwood Shark Cucullia artemisiae / abrotani (eats flowers).

ARTEMESIA MARITIMA, SEA WORMWOOD

Sole sustainer of 2: Essex Emerald Euchloris smaragdaria, and Scarce Pug Eupithecia extensaria.

Also sustains: Ground Lackey Malacosoma castrensis, Feathered Footman Coscinia striata / grammica (on seeds), and Bordered Pug Eupithecia succenturiata,

ARTEMESIA VULGARIS, MUGWORT

Sustains 9 Lepidoptera larva.

One of two sustainers occasionally, of second brood of Ash Pug Eupithecia innotata ssp. Fraxinata other being Fraxinus.

One of three sustainers Angle-barred Pug Eupithecia innotata (eats flowers) others being other Artemesia species.

Also sustains: Feathered Footman Coscinia striata / grammica (on seeds), Mouse Amphipyra tragopogonis, Mullein Wave Scopula marginepunctata / promutata / incanata, Wormwood Pug Eupithecia absinthiata / minutata, Bordered Pug Eupithecia succenturiata, Wormwood Shark Cucullia absinthii (seeds and buds), Tawny-speckled Pug Eupithecia icterata / subfulvata (eats flowers and seeds), and V Pug Chloroclystis coronata (eats flowers).

Arum maculatum, LORDS & LADIES, CUCKOO PINT

Arums sustain Lesser Broad-border Triphaena lanthina.

Asclepias species, MILKWEEDS

Flowers very rich in nectar.

Sole sustainer of the Monarch / Milkweed butterfly Danaus menippe / plexippus, which occassionally is blown here from the USA.

Asperula / Gallium odorata, WOODRUFF

Sustains 6 Lepidoptera larva: Flame Shoulder Ochropleura plecta, Cream Wave Scopula floslactata / remutata / remutaria, Dark-barred Twin-spot Carpet Xanthorhoe ferrugata / unidentaria, Red Twin-spot Carpet Xanthorhoe spadicearia / ferrugata, Green Carpet Colostygia pectinataria / viridaria, and Barred Straw Lygris pyraliata / dotata.

Aspidium filix-mas, MALE FERN

Sustains Small Angle-Shades Euplexia lucipara.

Aster tripolium, SEA ASTER / STARWORT

One of three sustainers Starwort Cucullia asteris (eats flowers) others being Callistephus and Solidago.

Also sustains Wormwood Pug Eupithecia absinthiata / minutata.

Astragalus glycphyllos, MILK-VETCH

One of three sustainers Black-neck Lygephila pastinum others being Lathyrus palustris and Vicia cracca.

Also sustains Scarce Black-neck Lygephila craccae.

Atriplex littoralis, SEA ORACHE

Sustains Ground Lackey Malacosoma castrensis.

Atriplex patula, COMMON ORACHE

Sustains 7 Lepidoptera larva: Lesser Broad-border Triphaena lanthina, Orache Trachea atriplicis, Nutmeg Hadena trifolii / chenopodii, Ground Lackey Malacosoma castrensis, Blood-vein Calothysanis amata / amataria, Dark Spinach Pelurga comitata (eats flowers and seeds), and Plain Pug Eupithecia subnotata / scabiosata (eats flowers and seeds).

Atriplex portulacoides, SEA PURSLANE

Sustains: Ground Lackey Malacosoma castrensis, Sand Dart Agrotis ripae, and Rosy Wave moth Scopula emutaria.

Atriplex sabulosa / laciniata, FROSTED ORACHE

Sustains Plain Pug Eupithecia subnotata (eats flowers and seeds).

Atropa belladonna, DEADLY NIGHTSHADE / DWALE

Poisonous

Sustains Death's-head Hawkmoth Acherontia atropos.

AURICULA SPECIES

Sustain Gothic Phalaena typica larvae (after hibernation).

AVENA SATIVA, OATS

<u>One of three sustainers</u> Flounced Rustic Luperina testacea (on roots) others being Hordeum and Triticum.

Also sustains: Rosy Minor Procus literosa (in stems), Rosy Rustic Hydraecia micacea (in stems), and Brighton Wainscot Oria musculosa (in stems).

AVENA UBESCENS, OAT-GRASS

Sustains: Beaded Chestnut Agrochola lychnidis / pistacina, and Dusky Sallow Eremobia ochroleuca (seeds).

AZALEA SPECIES

see also Ericaceae and Rhododendrons

Sustain Alder Apatele alni.

Suffers Leaf Miner moths Gracilaria azaleella under glass causing leaves to brown and drop as if scorched, often worst in the winter months the leaves may be distorted and folded around the cocoons.

BACILLUS THURINGIENSIS,

Naturally occurring disease of many Lepidoptera larva, now produced and sold commercially, against caterpillars on cabbages and related brassicas. In USA also used against tobacco bud and bollworms.

BALLOTA NIGRA, BLACK HOREHOUND

Sustains Wormwood Pug Eupithecia absinthiata / minutata.

BARBAREA VULGARIS, WINTER CRESS / YELLOW ROCKET

Flowers rich in nectar.

Suffers: badly from Green-veined White Pieris napi and Orange-Tip Anthocaris cardamines.

BARTSIA SPECIES

Semi-parasitic plants found on weeds in meadows.

One of two sustainers Barred Rivulet Perizoma bifaciata / unifasciata (mostly inside seed capsules) other being Euphrasia.

BELLIS PERENNIS, DAISY

Sustains: Orange Wainscot / Brown-line Bright-eye Leucania conigera, and Red Carpet moth Xanthorhoe munitata.

BERBERIS SPECIES,

-particularly wild BARBERRY, B. vulgaris

Flowers rich in nectar.

<u>Sole sustainers of 2</u>: Barberry Carpet Coenotephria berberata, and Scarce Tissue Calocalpe cervinalis / certata.

Also sustains: Pale-shouldered Brocade Hadena thalassina, and Mottled Pug Eupithecia exiguata.

BETA MARITIME, WILD BEET

Sustains Small Mottled Willow Laphygma exigua.

BETA VULGARIS, BEET / RED BEET / BEETROOT / LEAF BEAT / PERPETUAL SPINACH / SWISS CHARD / SUGAR BEET

Sustains two Lepidoptera larva Silver Gamma / Y Moth Plusia gamma, and Nutmeg Hadena trifolii / chenopodii.

BETONICA OFFICINALIS / STACHYS OFFICINALIS, BETONY

Sustains Portland Ribbon Wave Sterrha degeneraria.

BETULA ALBA, BIRCH

Sustains huge number, over 115 different Lepidoptera larva.

<u>Sole sustainer of 9</u>: Lesser Swallow Prominent Pheosia gnoma / dictaeoides, White Prominent Leucodonta bicoloria, Satin Lutestring Tethea fluctuosa, Yellow Horned Achlya flavicornis, Scalloped Hook-Tip Drepana lacertinaria / lacertula, Birch

Mocha Cosymbia albipunctata / pendularia, and Argent and Sable Eulype hastata, Orange Underwing Archiearis parthenias (on catkins first), and Rannoch Sprawler Brachyonycha nubeculosa (probably also eats other plants).

<u>One of two sustainers of 12</u>: Kentish Glory Endromis versicolora other being Alnus, Pebble Hook-Tip Drepana falcataria / falcula other being Alnus, Alder Kitten Harpyia bicuspis other being Alnus, Angle-Striped Sallow Enargia paleacea fulvago other being Populus tremula, Scarce Silver-Lines Pseudoips prasinana / bicolorana / quercana other being Quercus species, False Mocha Cosymbia punctaria other being Quercus species, Maiden's Blush Cosymbia punctaria other being Quercus species, Welsh Wave Venusia cambrica other being Sorbus aucuparia, Small Engrailed Ectropis crepuscularia / biundularia other being Larix, Brindled White Spot Ectropis extersaria / luridata other being Quercus species, Grey Birch Aethalura punctulata other being Alnus, and Speckled Beauty Alcis arenaria / angularia / viduata (on lichen on bark) other being that on Quercus species.

<u>One of three sustainers of 9</u>: Great Oak Beauty Boarmia roboraria others being Quercus and Salix species, Suspected Parastichtis suspecta others being Populus nigra and Salix species, Common Fanfoot Herminia barbalis others being Alnus and Quercus species, Treble Brown-spot Sterrha trigeminata / scutularia (eats flowers) others being Acer campestre and Hedera, Clouded Silver Bapta temerata / punctata others being Prunus padus and Prunus spinosa, Cousin German Triphaena sobrina others being Erica cinerea and Vaccinium myrtillus, Peacock Moth Semiothisa notata others being Salix alba and Salix caprea, Small Engrailed Ectropis bistortata / biundularia / laricaria / crepuscularia others being Carpinus and Ligustrum,

and Netted Mountain-Moth Isturgia carbonaria others being Arctostaphylos and Salix aurita.

Also sustains another 85: Pale Oak Beauty Boarmia punctinalis / consortaria, Northern Winter Moth Operophtera fagata / boreata, Camberwell Beauty Nymphalis antiopa, Hook-Tip Drepana lacertinaria, Lime Hawkmoth Mimas tiliae, Lobster Moth Stauropus fagi, Iron Prominent Notodonta dromedarius, Large Dark Prominent Notodonta torva, Coxcomb Prominent Lophopteryx capucina / camelina, Common Lutestring Tethea duplaris, Scarce Vapourer Orgyia recens / gonostigma, Dark Tussock Dasychira fascelina, Black V moth Leucoma v-nigrum / l-album, Pale Eggar Trichiura crataegii, December Moth Poecilo campapopuli, Small Eggar Eriogaster lanestris, Beautiful Brocade Hadena contigua, Golden-rod Brindle Lithomoia solidaginis, Satellite Eupsilia transversa / satellitia, Flounced Chestnut Anchocelis helvola / rufina, Miller Apatele leporina, Dark Dagger Apatele tridens, Scarce Dagger Apatele auricoma, Light Knotgrass Apatele menyanthidis, Sweet-Gale Apatele euphorbiae / myricae, Green Silver-Lines Bena fagana / prasinana, Nut-tree Tussock Colocasia coryli, Large Emerald Geometra papilionaria, Sussex Emerald Thalera fimbrialis, Little Emerald Iodis lactaearia, Clay Triple-lines Cosymbia linearia / trilinearia, Broken-barred Carpet Electrophaeus corylata, Blue-bordered Carpet Plemyria bicolorata / rubiginata, Red-green Carpet Chloroclysta siterata / psittacata, Autumn Green Carpet Chloroclysta miata, Common Marbled Carpet Dysstroma truncata / russata / centumnotata, Dark Marbled Carpet Dysstroma citrata / immanata, May Highflyer Hydriomena coerulata / impluviata / trifasciata, Early Tooth-striped Nothopteryx carpinata / lobulata, Autumnal Moth Oporinia autumnata, November Moth Oporinia dilutata / nebulata, Pale

November Moth Oporinia christyi, Small White Wave Asthena albulata / candida, Waved Carpet Hydrelia testaceata / sylvata, Common White Wave Cabera pusaria, Common Wave Cabera exanthemata, August Thorn Ennomos quercinaria / angularia, Canary-shouldered Thorn Deuteronomos alniaria / tiliaria, September Thorn Deuteronomos erosaria, Lunar Thorn Selenia lunaria, Scorched Wing Plagodis dolobraria, Dark Bordered Beauty Epione vespertaria / parallelaria, Small Brindled Beauty Apocheima hispidaria, Ringed Carpet Cleora cinctaria, Square-Spot Ectropis consonaria, Swallow Prominent Notodonta / Pheosia dictaea, Red-necked Footman Atolmis rubricollis (green algae on bark and dead wood), Buff Footman Eilema deplana (green algae on bark and dead wood), Large / Four-spotted Footman Lithosia quadra (lichen and algae on bark and dead wood), and Olive Crescent Trisateles emortualis (dead birch leaves and lichens).

In spring after hibernation sustains: Double Dart Graphiphora augur, Purple Clay Diarsia brunnea, Triple-spotted Clay Amathes ditrapezium, Silvery Arches Polia hepatica / tincta, Green Arches Anaplectoides prasina / herbida, Great Brocade Eurois occulta, Broad-bordered Yellow Underwing Lampra fimbriata / fimbria, Grey Arches Polia nebulosa, Copper Underwing Amphipyra pyramidea, Old Lady Mormo maura, Common Emerald Hemithea aestivaria / strigata / thymiaria, Scarce Umber Eriannis aurantiara, Occasionally sustains: Muslin Cycnia mendica (usually found on herbaceous plants), Small Angle-Shades Euplexia lucipara, Blossom Underwing Orthosia miniosa, Poplar Kitten Harpyia hermelina, Scarce Marveil (sic) -du-Jour Moma alpion / orion.

Suffers: Buff-Tip Phalera bucephala, Yellow / Gold Tail Euproctis similes / auriflua, Black Arches Lymantria monacha, Emperor

Saturnia pavonia / carpini, Hebrew Character Orthosia gothica, Pale Pinion Lithophane socia / petrificata, and Grey Dagger Apatele psi.

BORAGO OFFICINALIS, BORAGE

Sustains: Queen of Spain Fritillary Argynnis lathonia, Crimson-speckled Utetheisa pulchella, and may sustain Bright Wave Sterrha ochrata / ochrearia.

BRACHYPODIUM PINNATUM, HEATH FALSE-BROME GRASS

Sustains 7 Lepidoptera larva.

Sole sustainer of Lulworth Skipper Thymelicus action / actaeon.

One of two sustainers Straw Dot Rivula sericealis other being Carex.

One of three sustainers Essex Skipper Thymelicus lineola others being Agropyron repens and Phleum.

Also sustains: Grayling Satyrus semele, Meadow Brown Maniola jurtina / janira, Small Heath Coenonympha pamphilus, and Small Skipper Thymelicus sylvestris / linea / thaumus.

BRACHYPODIUM SYLVATICUM, SLENDER FALSE-BROME GRASS

Sustains 8 Lepidoptera larva.

One of two sustainers of 2: Chequered Skipper Carterocephalus palaemon / paniscus other being Bromus, and Straw Dot Rivula sericealis other being Carex.

Also sustains: Speckled Wood / Wood Argus Pararge negeria, Wall butterfly Pararge megera, Ringlet Aphantopus hyperantus, Large Skipper Ochlodes venata / sylvanus, Small Skipper Thymelicus sylvestris / linea / thaumus, and Feathered Ear Pachetra sagittigera / leucophaea.

BRASSICAS

Sustain / suffer a huge number of Lepidoptera larva: Silver Y moth Autographa gamma, Dot moth Melanchra persicariae, Flax tortrix moth Cnephasia interjectana, Tomato moth / Bright-line Brown-eye moth Lacanobia oleracea, Turnip moth Agrotis segetum, Garden Pebble moth Evergestis forficalis, Bright Wave Sterrha ochrata / ochrearia, Pearly Underwing Peridroma saucia, Garden Carpet moth Xanthorhoe fluctuata, Heart & Dart moth Agrotis exclamationis, Dark Swordgrass / Dark Dart Agrotis ipsilon, and fat, black striped larvae of Great Yellow Underwing Moth Noctua / Tryphaena pronuba (on roots and leaves).

Suffer: the Large Cabbage White Pieris brassicae, which has black markings on creamy white wings, these lay yellow eggs in clusters of thirty to a hundred, caterpillars start greyish green but may become bright green with black markings or bluish green with three lines yellow and black spots when mature, they quit the plants to pupate nearby, the butterflies are deterred by tomatoes, thyme and by fake eggs or crushed eggs. Parasitised by small black braconid wasp Apanteles glomeratus, this lays eggs in caterpillar which eventually form up to thirty yellow cocoons around the poor critter having eaten it from the inside. However these are themselves parasitized by hyper-parasites, an even smaller metallic green wasp Tetrastichus galactopus and an Ichneumon wasp Lysibia nana. Apantales cocoons may be conflated with small yellow silky cocoons containing pupae of the Ichneumon fly Microgaster glomeratus who lays about sixty eggs in a Large White caterpillar parasitising it. Another Ichneumon Fly Pteromalus brassicae lays up to two hundred and fifty eggs on the newly formed chrysalis parasitizing it. These Lepidoptera caterpillars can be controlled with Bacillus thuriengiensis, found naturally in the soil or available commercially. As these caterpillars mostly damage the outer leaves they can do more harm to such as kales (which they seldom touch) and Portugese cabbage, Trouve conchuda, while with cabbage, cauliflower and broccolis the heads may escape almost unscathed, though obviously growing less well when the leaf area removed is significant.

Suffer the similar Small White or Turnip Moth Artogeia / Pieris rapae, their eggs are laid singly becoming velvet green caterpillars with three yellow lines and NO black spots.

Suffer the Green Veined White P. napi, their eggs laid singly, grub velvet green with a row of red to yellow breathing holes on sides. These both do much damage to the heads of cabbage, cauliflowers, broccolli as they eat into the middle. More of these caterpillars will be found on plants growing on their own than on those in stands of many.

Suffer the Cabbage moth Mamestra brassicae whose fat brown caterpillars eat the inside of the heart each causing far more damage than other caterpillars which consume mostly outer leaves, the eggs are laid singly so hard to spot though the grub's greenish brown frass is easily found.

Also suffer the Diamond-back moth Plutella xylostella which has grey green caterpillars which feed on the leaf underside leaving the thin transparent upper skin and veins, these reach about half an inch long then pupate in cocoons on the leaves before emerging to start the next, of up to ten generations in a year.

BRIZA MEDIA, COMMON QUAKING-GRASS

Sustains Slender Brindle Apamea scolopacina.

BRIZA MINOR, LESSER QUAKING-GRASS

Sustains Slender Brindle Apamea scolopacina.

BROMUS ARVENSIS, FIELD BROME-GRASS

Sustains Shaded Broad-Bar Ortholitha chenopodiata / limitata / mensuraria, Wall butterfly Pararge megera, Marbled White Melanargia galathea, and Meadow Brown Maniola jurtina.

BROMUS RAMOSUS, ROUGH BROME-GRASS

One of two sustainers Chequered Skipper Carterocephalus palaemon / paniscus other being Brachypodium.

Also sustains: Wall butterfly Pararge megera, Marbled White Melanargia galathea, and Meadow Brown Maniola jurtina.

BUDDLEIA / BUDDLEIJA DAVIDII, BUTTERFLY BUSH

Flowers, blueish, rich in nectar, legendary for attracting butterflies, also a self seeding weed and very invasive so has recently populated almost every waste ground and railway track in the UK.

BUDDLEIA GLOBOSA

Flowers, orange, smaller than B. davidii though still rich in nectar, but this species does not self seed like B. davidii.

Sustains Mullein Shark Cucullia verbasci.

BUTTERFLIES, UNWANTED

Because the following caterpillar / larva / worm / grub, is either effectively or nearly polyphagous or omnivorous then almost any plant may unwillingly sustain great unwanted plagues, however on others they are just occasional.

The worst of these are almost completely polyphagous (eat almost anything), even the catfood is not safe: Garden Tiger Arctia caia, Cream-spot Tiger Arctia villica, Jersey Tiger Euplagia quadripunctaria / hera, Large Yellow Underwing Triphaena pronuba, Angle-Shades Phlogophora meticulosa, and Grey Pug Eupithecia castigata.

The following are predominantly **herbaceous plant** devourers, but will tackle almost any plant: Striped Hawkmoth Celerio livornica, White Ermine Spilosoma lubricipeda / menthastri, Buff Ermine Spilosoma lutea / lubricipeda, Garden Dart Euxoa nigricans, White-line Dart Euxoa tritici / aquilina, Turnip Moth Agrotis segetum, Cabbage Moth Mamestra brassicae, Broom Moth Ceramica pisi, Swordgrass Xylena exsoleta, Red Swordgrass Xylena vetusta, Beautiful Arches Eumichtus satura, Large Ranunculus Antitype flavicincta, Grey Chi moth Antitype chi, Brown Rustic Rusina umbratica / tenebrosa, Old Lady Mormo maura, Mottled Rustic Caradrina morpheus, Scarce Bordered Straw Heliothis armigera, Ni Plusia ni, Silver Y Plusia gamma, Isle of Wight Wave Sterrha humiliata / osseata, Satyr Pug Eupithecia satyrata, Belted Beauty Nyssia zonaria, and Hay Moth / Pale Mottled Willow Caradrina quadripunctata.

These following are predominantly **deciduous tree and shrub devourers** but will also tackle almost any plant: Light Emerald Campaea margaritata, Large Thorn Ennomos autumnaria / alniaria, Buff Tip Phalera bucephala, Vapourer Orgyia antiqua, Pale Tussock Dasychira pudibunda, Gipsy Moth Lymantria dispar, Black Arches Lymantria monacha, Lackey Malacosoma neustria, Dot Melanchra persicariae, Hebrew Character Orthosia gothica, Pale Pinion Lithophane socia / petrificata, Dun-bar Cosmia trapezina (apparently will also eat cooked mutton), March-moth Alsophila aescularia, Small Dusty Wave Sterrha seriata / incanata / virgularia, Winter moth Operophtera brumata, Early Thorn Selenia bilunaria / illunaria, Purple Thorn Selenia tetralunaria / illustraria, Scalloped Hazel Gonodontis bidentata, Feathered Thorn Colotois pennaria, Scalloped Oak Crocallis elinguaria, Orange moth Angerona prunaria, Swallow-tailed moth Ourapteryx sambucaria, Dotted Border Erannis marginaria / progemmaria, Mottled Umber Erannis defoliaria, Pale Brindled Beauty Phigalia pedaria / pilosaria, Brindled Beauty Lycia hirtaria, Peppered moth Biston betularia, Oak Beauty Biston strataria / prodromaria, Willow Beauty Alcis rhomboidaria / gemmaria, and Mottled Beauty Alcis repandata.

BUXUS SEMPERVIRENS, BOX
Sustains Satin Beauty moth Deileptenia ribeata / abietaria.

CAKILE MARITIME, SEA ROCKET

Sustains Sand Dart Agrotis ripae.

CALAMAGROSTIS EPIGEIOS, BUSH-GRASS

Sole sustainer of Concolorous Arenostola extrema / concolor (in stem).

One of two sustainers Mere Wainscot Arenostola fluxa / helmanni (in stem) other being C. canescens.

Also sustains Ringlet Aphantopus hyperantus.

CALAMAGROSTIS CANESCENS, PURPLE SMALL-REED

One of two sustainers of Mere Wainscot Arenostola fluxa / helmanni (in stem) other being C. epigeios.

CALENDULA OFFICINALIS, POT MARIGOLD

Sustains Bordered Straw Heliothis peltigera (mostly eats flowers and seeds), Mamestra brassicae Cabbage moth.

CALLISTEPHUS HORTENSIS / CHINENSIS, CHINA ASTER

One of three sustainers Starwort Cucullia asteris (eats flowers) others being Aster and Solidago.

CALLUNA VULGARIS, LING HEATHER

Flowers rich in nectar.

Sustains 41 Lepidoptera larva.

Sole sustainer of 4: White-line Snout Schrankia taenialis / albistrigalis (flowers), Arran Carpet Dysstroma concinnata, Narrow-winged Pug Eupithecia nanata, and Horse-chestnut Pachycnemia hippocastanaria.

One of two sustainers of 2: True Lover's Knot Lycophotia varia / porphyrea / strigula other being Erica cinerea, and Beautiful Yellow Underwing Anarta myrtilli other being Erica cinerea.

One of 3 sustainers of 6: Heath Rustic Amathes agathina others being Erica cinerea and Erica tetralix, Scarce Silver Y Plusia interrogationis others being Vaccinium myrtillus and Vaccinium uliginosum, Weaver's Wave Sterrha churnata / contiguaria others being Cotyledon and Empetrum, Small Autumnal / Carpet Oporinia filigrammaria others being Saxafraga aizoides and Vaccinum myrtillus, Bordered Grey Selidosema plumaria / ericetaria others being Sarothamnus and Trifoliums, and Grey Scalloped Bar Dyscia fagaria others being Erica cinerea and Erica tetralix.

Also sustains: Silver-Studded Blue Phlebius argus / aegon, Dark Tussock Dasychira fascelina, Pale Eggar Trichiura crataegii, Oak Eggar Lasiocampa quercus, Fox moth Macrothylacia rubi, Feathered Footman Coscinia striata / grammica, Speckled Footman Coscinia cribraria / cribrum, Great Brocade Eurois occulta, Lesser Yellow Underwing Triphaena comes / orbona, Deep Brown Dart Aporophyla lutulenta, Golden-rod Brindle Lithomoia solidaginis, Light Knotgrass Apatele menyanthidis, Sweet-Gale Apatele euphorbiae / myricae, Small Grass Emerald Chlorissa viridata, Lewes Wave Scopula immorata, Lead Belle Ortholitha mucronata / plumbaria / palumbaria, Grey Mountain Carpet Entephria caesiata, Common Marbled Carpet Dysstroma

truncata / russata / centumnotata, Dark Marbled Carpet
Dysstroma citrata / immanata, July Highflyer Hydriomena
furcata / elutata / sordidata, Ling Pug Eupithecia goossensiata /
minutata (flowers and seeds), Magpie Abraxas grossulariata,
Rannoch Brindled Beauty Poccilopsis lapponaria, Annulet
Gnophos obscurata / pullata, Scotch Annulet Gnophos myrtillata
/ obfuscaria, Common Heath-moth Ematurga atomaria, Grass
Wave Perconia strigillaria, Green Hairstreak Callophrys rubi
(flowers and leaves), and probably Dark Brocade Eumichtis
adusta.

CAMPANULA GLOMERATA, CLUSTERED BELLFLOWER

Sustains: Wormwood Pug Eupithecia absinthiata / minutata, and
Lime-speck Pug Eupithecia centaureata / oblongata (flowers).

CAMPANULA ROTUNDIFLOIA, HAREBELL

Sustains: Northern Rustic Ammogrotis lucernea, Ashworth's
Rustic Amathes ashworthii, and Black-Banded Antitype
xanthomista / nigrocincta (flowers and seeds).

CAMPANULA TRACHELIUM, NETTLE-LEAVED BELLFLOWER

Sole sustainer of Campanula Pug Eupithecia denotata /
campanulata (seeds and capsules).

CARDAMINE BULBIFERA, CORAL-ROOT

Sustains Silver Washed Fritillary Argynnis paphia.

Cardamine pratensis, CUCKOO-FLOWER / LADY'S SMOCK/ BITTERCRESS

Sustains / suffers: Green-veined White Pieris napi, and Orange-Tip Anthocaris cardamines.

Carduus acanthoides, THISTLE

Blooms recorded visited by 44 different insect species: 4 butterflies and moths, 32 species bee, 3 species Diptera flies and 5 others, another reference says of every hundred visitors to the flowers 27% are butterflies and moths, 58% are bees, and 12% flies.

Sustains Belted Beauty Nyssia zonaria.

Also sustains 3 other larva on the flowerheads which also eat gall fly larvae: Phycitodes binaevella, Eucosma cana and Myelois cribrella.

Carduus arvensis, CREEPING THISTLE

Blooms visited by 88 unspecified insect species.

Sustains: Painted Lady Vanessa cardui, Belted Beauty Nyssia zonaria.

Also sustains 3 other larva on the flowerheads which also eat gall fly larvae: Phycitodes binaevella, Eucosma cana and Myelois cribrella.

Carduus crispus, WELTED THISTLE

Sustains: Painted Lady Vanessa cardui, and Belted Beauty Nyssia zonaria.

Also sustains 3 other larva on the flowerheads which also eat gall fly larvae: Phycitodes binaevella, Eucosma cana and Myelois cribrella.

CARDUUS LANCEOLATUS, SPEAR THISTLE

Blooms visited by 12 insect species.

Sustains: Painted Lady Vanessa cardui, Burnished Brass Plusia chrysitis, and Belted Beauty Nyssia zonaria.

Also sustains 3 other larva on the flowerheads which also eat gall fly larvae: Phycitodes binaevella, Eucosma cana and Myelois cribrella.

CARDUUS NUTANS, MUSK / NODDING THISTLE

Sustains: Painted Lady Vanessa cardui, Frosted Orange Gortyna flavago / ochracea (in stems), and Belted Beauty Nyssia zonaria.

Also sustains 3 other larva on the flowerheads which also eat gall fly larvae: Phycitodes binaevella, Eucosma cana and Myelois cribrella.

CARDUUS PALUSTRIS, MARSH THISTLE

Blooms visited by 22 insect species.

Sustains: Frosted Orange Gortyna flavago / ochracea (in stems), and Belted Beauty Nyssia zonaria.

Also sustains 3 other larva on the flowerheads which also eat gall fly larvae: Phycitodes binaevella, Eucosma cana and Myelois cribrella.

CAREX ACUTIFORMIS, MARSH SEDGE

Sole sustainer of Dusky Ear Sedina buttneri (in stems).

One of two sustainers Straw Dot Rivula sericealis other being Brachypodium.

Also sustains: Large Heath / Marsh Ringlet Coenonympha tullia / davus / tiphon, Vapourer Orgyia antiqua, Red Swordgrass Xylena vetusta, and Crescent Celaena leucostigma / fibrosa (in stems).

Carex caespitosa, TUFTED SEDGE

One of three sustainers Reed Dagger / Powdered Wainscot Simyra albovenosa / venosa others being Phragmites australis and Poa aquatica.

One of two sustainers Straw Dot Rivula sericealis other being Brachypodium.

Also sustains: Large Heath / Marsh Ringlet Coenonympha tullia / davus / tiphon, Vapourer Orgyia antiqua, Red Swordgrass Xylena vetusta, Smoky Wainscot Leucania impure, Small Wainscot Arenostola pygmina / fulva (in flower stem), and Gold Spot Plusia festucae.

Carex flacca, GLAUCOUS SEDGE

Sole sustainer of Least Minor Phothedes captiuncula / expolita (in stems).

One of two sustainers Straw Dot Rivula sericealis other being Brachypodium.

Also sustains: Large Heath / Marsh Ringlet Coenonympha tullia / davus / tiphon, Vapourer Orgyia antiqua, Red Swordgrass Xylena vetusta, Gold Spot Plusia festucae, Rosy Minor Procus literosa (in stems), and Small Wainscot Arenostola pygmina / fulva (in flower stem).

CAREX PANICEA, CARNATION SEDGE

<u>One of two sustainers</u> Straw Dot Rivula sericealis other being Brachypodium.

Also sustains: Gold Spot Plusia festucae, Large Heath / Marsh Ringlet Coenonympha tullia / davus / tiphon, Vapourer Orgyia antiqua, and Red Swordgrass Xylena vetusta.

CAREX SYLVATICA WOOD SEDGE

<u>Sole sustainer of</u> Silver Hook Eustrotia uncula / uncana / unca though possibly eats other sedges.

<u>One of two sustainers</u> Straw Dot Rivula sericealis other being Brachypodium.

<u>One of three sustainers</u> Dotted Fanfoot Zanclognatha cribrumalis / cribralis (in stems also eats leaves) others being Luzula species.

Also sustains: Large Heath / Marsh Ringlet Coenonympha tullia / davus / tiphon, Vapourer Orgyia antiqua, Red Swordgrass Xylena vetusta, Ringlet butterfly Aphantopus hyperantus, and Gold Spot Plusia festucae.

CAREX VESICARIA, BLADDER SEDGE

<u>One of two sustainers</u> Straw Dot Rivula sericealis other being Brachypodium.

Also sustains Gold Spot Plusia festucae, Large Heath / Marsh Ringlet Coenonympha tullia / davus / tiphon, Vapourer Orgyia antiqua, and Red Swordgrass Xylena vetusta.

Carlina vulgaris, CARLINE THISTLE

<u>One of two sustainers</u> Purple Marbled Eublemma ostrina other being Echinops.

Also sustains Painted Lady Vanessa cardui.

Carpinus betulus, HORNBEAM

Sustains 15 Lepidoptera larva.

<u>One of three sustainers</u> Small / Engrailed Ectropis bistortata / biundularia / laricaria / crepuscularia others being Betula and Ligustrum.

Also sustains: Coxcomb Prominent Lophopteryx capucina / camelina, Purple Clay Diarsia brunnea (in spring), Dotted Clay Amathes baia (in spring), Barred Sallow Tiliacea aurago, Nut-tree Tussock Colocasia coryli, Little Emerald Iodis lactaearia, Red-green Carpet Chloroclysta siterata / psittacata, November Moth Oporinia dilutata / nebulata, Small White Wave Asthena albulata / candidata, Scarce Umber Eriannis aurantiara, Small Brindled Beauty Apocheima hispidaria, Square-Spot Ectropis consonaria, Buff-Tip Phalera bucephala, and Emperor Saturnia pavonia / carpini.

Carum carvi, CARAWAY

Blossoms recorded as visited by 55 species of insect: 1 butterfly, 9 species bee, 21 species Diptera flies and 24 others.

Sustains Swallow-tail Papilio machaon.

Castanea sativa, SWEET CHESTNUT

<u>One of three sustainers</u> Purple Hairstreak Thecla quercus others being Quercus and Salix species.

Cedrus species, CEDARS

<u>One of two sustainers</u> Pine Carpet Thera firmata the other being Pinus.

Centaurea cyanus, CORNFLOWER

Sustains Black-veined Moth Siona lineata / dealbata.

Centaurea jacea / nigra / nemoralis, (continental / UK / dwarf sub-species) KNAPWEED / LESSER KNAPWEED

Blooms visited by at least 48 different insect species: 13 butterflies and moths, 28 species bee, 6 species Diptera flies and 1 other, another says of every hundred visitors to the flowers 27% butterflies and moths, 58% are bees, and 12 flies. And yet another reference gives 84 species taking nectar and or pollen: 20 butterflies and moths, 2 beetles, 28 bees and wasps, 34 flies, with another 10 species visiting for some reason while apparently not taking nectar or pollen: 2 butterflies and moths, 5 beetles, 2 bees and wasps, 1 fly, perhaps these visit to predate some of the others.

Sustains 5 Lepidoptera larva; Belted Beauty Nyssia zonaria, Black-veined Moth Siona lineata / dealbata, Marbled Clover Heliothis dipsacea / viriplaca (eats flowers and seeds), Satyr Pug Eupithecia satyrata (eats flowers), and Eucosma cana (in flowerheads).

CENTAUREA SCABIOSA, GREATER KNAPWEED

Blooms visited by 21 insect species.

Sustains Scarce Forester Ino globulariae.

CENTRANTHUS RUBER, FALSE VALERIAN

Red pink flowers beloved by butterflies.

CERASTIUM ARVENSE FIELD MOUSE-EAR CHICKWEED

<u>One of two sustainers</u> Marsh Pug Eupithecia palustraria / pygmaeata (eats flowers) other being Stellaria.

Also sustains: Ruby Tiger Spilosoma / Phragmatobia fuliginosa, and possibly Portland Ribbon Wave Sterrha degeneraria, and Small Yellow Underwing Panemeria tenebrata / arbuti (flowers and seeds).

CERASTIUM SEMIDECANDRUM, LITTLE MOUSE-EAR CHICKWEED

Sustains: White-line Dart Euoxa tritici / aquilina, Ruby Tiger Spilosoma / Phragmatobia fuliginosa, possibly Portland Ribbon Wave Sterrha degeneraria, and Small Yellow Underwing Panemeria tenebrata / arbuti (flowers and seeds).

CERASTIUM VISCOSUM, VISCID MOUSE-EAR CHICKWEED

<u>One of two sustainers</u> Cloaked Carpet Euphyia picata other being Stellarias.

Also sustains: Ruby Tiger Spilosoma / Phragmatobia fuliginosa, and possibly Portland Ribbon Wave Sterrha degeneraria, Coast

Dart Euoxa cursoria, White-line Dart Euoxa tritici / aquilina, and Small Yellow Underwing Panemeria tenebrata / arbuti (flowers and seeds).

CERASTIUM VULGATUM, MOUSE-EAR CHICKWEED

Sustains Small Yellow Underwing Panemeria tenebrata / arbuti (flowers and seeds), Ruby Tiger Spilosoma / Phragmatobia fuliginosa, and possibly Portland Ribbon Wave Sterrha degeneraria.

CHAENOMELES JAPONICA / SPECIOSA, JAPANESE QUINCE

Sustains Figure of Eight Episema caeruleocephala.

CHEIRANTHUS CHEIRI, WALLFLOWERS

Sustain Garden Carpet moth Xanthorhoe fluctuata.

Suffers Angle Shades moth Phogophora meticulosa (leaves, flowerbuds and blooms).

CHENOPODIUM ALBUM, FAT HEN / WHITE GOOSEFOOT

Sustains 13 Lepidoptera larva: Heart & Club Agrotis clavis / corticea, Heart & Dart Agrotis exclamationis, Dark Swordgrass Agrotis ipsilon / suffusa, Flame Axylia putris, Nutmeg Hadena trifolii / chenopodii, Brown Brocade / Bright-line Brown Eye Diataraxia oleracea, Orache Trachea atriplicis, Mottled Rustic Caradrina morpheus, Spotted Clover Heliothis scutosa (eats flowers and leaves), Dark Spinach Pelurga comitata (flowers and seeds), Plain Pug Eupithecia subnotata (flowers and seeds), and possible sustainer Dotted-Border Wave Sterrha sylvestraria / straminata.

CHENOPODIUM BONUS-HENRICUS, GOOD KING HENRY

Sustains: Nutmeg Hadena trifolii / chenopodii, Orache Trachea atriplicis, Dark Spinach Pelurga comitata (eats flowers and seeds), and Plain Pug Eupithecia subnotata (flowers and seeds).

CHENOPODIUM RUBRUM, RED GOOSEFOOT

Sustains: Sand Dart Agrotis ripae, and Nutmeg Hadena trifolii / chenopodii.

CHENOPODIUM VULVARIA, STINKING GOOSEFOOT

Sustains 6 Lepidoptera larvae: Brown Brocade / Bright-line Brown Eye Diataraxia oleracea, Nutmeg Hadena trifolii / chenopodii, Orache Trachea atriplicis, Mottled Rustic Caradrina morpheus, Dark Spinach Pelurga comitata (eats flowers and seeds), and Plain Pug Eupithecia subnotata (flowers and seeds).

CHRYSANTHEMUM GARDEN FORMS

Sustain: Gem moth Nycterosea obstipata / fluviata / gemmata, and Satyr Pug Eupithecia satyrata (eats flowers).

Suffers: several Tortrix moths, Angle Shades Phlogophora meticulosa, Gothic Phalaena typica, Cabbage moth Mamestra brassicae, and Turnip moth Agrotis segetum.

CHRYSANTHEMUM LEUCANTHEMUM, OX EYE DAISY

Blooms attract 72 different insect species with long flowering period: 5 butterflies and moths, 12 species bee, 28 species flies and 27 others.

Sustains Cinnabar moth Callimorpha jacobaea.

CHRYSANTHEMUM PARTHENIUM, FEVERFEW

Sustains Chamomile Shark Cucullia chamomillae (eats flowers).

CICHORIUM INTYBUS, CHICORY / SUCCORY

Sustains: Feathered Footman Coscinia striata / grammica, Feathered Brindle Aporophyla australis, and Marbled Clover Heliothis dipsacea /viriplaca (eats flowers and seeds).

CICUTA VIROSA, COWBANE

Sustains: Wormwood Pug Eupithecia absinthiata / minutata, Reed Wainscot Nonagria algae / cannae (in stem), and Lime-speck Pug Eupithecia centaureata / oblongata (eats flowers).

CINERARIA SPP. DUSTY MILLER

Suffers Angle Shades Moth Phlogophora meticulosa.

CIRCAEA LUTETIANA, ENCHANTER'S NIGHTSHADE

One of three sustainers Small Phoenix Ecliptopera silaceata others being Epilobium species.

Also sustains Elephant Hawkmoth Deilephila elpenor.

CIRSIUM ARVENSE, THISTLES

Blooms visited by 88 different insect species: 7 butterflies and moths, 32 species bee, 24 species flies and 25 others.

Sustains 18 Lepidoptera larva.

Sustains: Belted Beauty Nyssia zonaria, Painted Lady Cynthia cardui, Silver Y Autographa gamma, and Swordgrass Xylena exsoleta.

Plus. Numerous small moth caterpillars (some of which may also eat gall fly larvae as well as foliage and or flower parts): Agapeta hamana, Aethes cnicana, A. rubigana, Lobesia abscisana, Eucosma cana, Homeosoma nebulella, Coleophora peribenanderi, Scrobipalpa acuminatella, Epiblema scutulana, Agonopterix subpropinquella, A. arenella, Phycitodes binavella, Sitochroa verticalis, and Myelois cribrella (in stems).

CIRSIUM ERIOPHORUM
Sustains Myelois cribrella (in stems).

CIRSIUM VULGARE
Sustains Agonopterix arenella.

Also sustains Myelois cribrella (in stems), Eucosma cana (in flowerhead), Homoeosoma nebulella (in flowerhead) and Phycitodes binaevella (which may also eat any gall fly larvae as well).

CLADIUM MARISCUS, COMMON FEN-SEDGE
One of three sustainers Reed Tussock Laelia caenosa others being Phragmites australis and Sparganium.

Also sustains: Red Swordgrass Xylena vetusta, and Crescent Celaena leucostigma / fibrosa (inside stems).

CLEMATIS VITALBA, TRAVELLER'S JOY

Native. Flowers rich in nectar. Garden Clematis of other species may possibly be able to sustain some larvae.

Sustains 11 Lepidoptera larva.

<u>Sole sustainer of 4</u>: Small Emerald Hemistola immaculate / vernaria / chrysoprasaria, Pretty Chalk Carpet Melanthia procellata (thought to seldom attack garden species), Small Waved Umber Horisme vitalbata, and Haworth's Pug Eupithecia haworthiata / isogrammaria (in flower-buds).

Also sustains: Sub-angled Wave Scopula nigropunctata / strigilaria, Fern Horisme tersata, Wormwood Pug Eupithecia absinthiata / minutata, Orange Moth Angerona prunaria, Lime-speck Pug Eupithecia centaureata / oblongata (eats flowers), V Pug Chloroclystis coronata (flowers), and Double-striped Pug Gymnoscelis pumilata (flowers).

COLUTEA ARBORESCENS, BLADDER SENNA

Flowers are rich in nectar.

Sustains Long Tailed Blue Lampides boeticus (flowers and seeds).

CONOPODIUM DENUDATUM, EARTHNUT

<u>One of two sustainers</u> Chimney Sweeper Odezia atrata (eats flowers) other being Anthriscus.

Convallaria majalis, LILY OF THE VALLEY
Sustains Grey Chi moth Antitype chi.

Convolvulus arvensis FIELD / LESSER BINDWEED
Sustains 10 Lepidoptera larvae.

<u>Sole sustainer of 2</u>: Spotted Sulphur Emmelia trabealis / sulphuralis, and Tawny Wave Scopula rubiginata / rubricata.

<u>One of two sustainers</u> Convovulus Hawkmoth Herse convolvuli other below.

<u>One of three sustainers of 2</u>: Pale Shoulder Tarache solaris / lucida others being Glechoma and Malvas, and Four-Spotted Acontia luctuosa others being Malvas and Plantagos.

Also sustains: Small Scallop Sterrha emarginata, Double-striped Pug Gymnoscelis pumilata (flowers), and occasionally Elephant Hawkmoth Deilephila elpenor. Possible sustainer Portland Ribbon Wave Sterrha degeneraria.

Sustains / Suffers Gem moth Nycterosea obstipata / fluviata / gemmata.

Convolvulus sepium GREATER BINDWEED
<u>One of two sustainers</u> Convolvulus Hawkmoth Herse convolvuli other being C. arvensis

Also sustains: Rosy Wave moth Scopula emutaria, occasionally sustains Elephant Hawkmoth Deilephila elpenor. Possible sustainer Portland Ribbon Wave Sterrha degeneraria.

Sustains / Suffers Gem moth Nycterosea obstipata / fluviata / gemmata.

Convolvulus soldanella, SEA BINDWEED

<u>One of three sustainers</u> White Colon Heliophobus albicolon(flowers) others being Sisymbrium sophia and Ononis arvensis.

Also sustains: Sand Dart Agrotis ripae, Portland Moth Actebia praecox, and Bordered Straw Heliothis peltigera (mostly eats flowers and seeds).

Cornus mas, CORNELIAN CHERRY

<u>One of three sustainers</u> Oleander Hawkmoth Daphnis nerii others being Nerium and Vincas.

Cornus sanguinea, CORNEL / DOGWOOD

Sustain 11 Lepidoptera larva: Death's-head Hawkmoth Acherontia atropos, Oak Eggar Lasiocampa quercus, Broad-bordered Yellow Underwing Lampra fimbriata / fimbria (after hibernation), Little Emerald Iodis lactaearia, Mottled Pug Eupithecia exiguata, Little Thorn Cepphis advenaria, Cream-spot Tiger Arctia villica, Holly / Azure Blue Celastrina argiolus (eats flowers and flower buds and green berries as well as leaves), Yellow-barred Brindle Acasis viretata (flowers first, then green berries then leaves), Green Hairstreak Callophrys rubi (flowers as well as leaves), and occasionally Privet Hawkmoth Sphinx ligustri.

Corylus avellana, HAZEL / COB / FILBERT

Sustain 31 Lepidoptera larva.

<u>One of three sustainers</u> Clouded Magpie Abraxas sylvata / ulmata others being Fagus and Ulmus.

Also sustains: Lime Hawkmoth Mimas tiliae, Lobster Moth Stauropus fagi, Iron Prominent Notodonta dromedaries, Coxcomb Prominent Lophopteryx capucina / camelina, Common Lutestring Tethea duplaris, Scarce Vapourer Orgyia recens / gonostigma, Pale Eggar Trichiura crataegii, Broad-bordered Yellow Underwing Lampra fimbriata / fimbria (after hibernation), Beautiful Brocade Hadena contigua, Small Quaker Orthosia cruda / pulverulenta, Sprawler Brachyonycha sphinx / cassinia, Coronet Craniophora ligustri, Green Silver-Lines Bena fagana / prasinana, Nut-tree Tussock Colocasia coryli, Large Emerald Geometra papilionaria, Little Emerald Iodis lactaearia, July Highflyer Hydriomena furcata / elutata / sordidata, Autumnal Moth Oporinia autumnata, November Moth Oporinia dilutata / nebulata, Small White Wave Asthena albulata / candidata, Magpie Abraxas grossulariata, Clouded Border Lomaspilis marginata, Common White Wave Cabera pusaria, Brimstone Moth Opisthograptis luteolata / crataegata, Bordered Beauty Epione repandaria / apiciaria, Buff-Tip Phalera bucephala, Emperor Saturnia pavonia / carpini, Swordgrass Xylena exsoleta, occasionally Blossom Underwing Orthosia miniosa, and Green Hairstreak Callophrys rubi (catkins).

COTONEASTER SPECIES
Copious whitish flowers are rich in nectar.

Sustains: Green-Brindled Crescent Allophyes oxyaercanthae, Figure of Eight Episema caeruleocephala, and Purple Thorn Selenia tetralunaria / illustraria.

COTYLEDON UMBILICUS, WALL PENNYWORT (SIC) / NAVELWORT

<u>One of three sustainers</u> Weaver's Wave Sterrha churnata / contiguaria others being Calluna vulgaris and Empetrum.

Also sustains Magpie Abraxas grossulariata.

CRATAEGUS OXYCANTHA, QUICKTHORN / HAWTHORN / MAY

Sustains 73 Lepidoptera larva.

<u>Sole sustainer of</u> Clay Fanfoot Paracolax derivalis (which may later complete cycle eating almost any form of undergrowth).

<u>One of two sustainers of 4</u>: Marsh Dagger Apatele strigosa other being Prunus spinosa, Pinion-spotted Pug Eupithecia insigniata / consignata other being Malus, Oak-tree Pug Eupithecia dodoneata other being Quercus species, and White Pinion-spotted Bapta bimaculata / taminata other being Prunus avium.

<u>One of three sustainers</u> Early Moth Theria rupicapraria others being Vaccinium myrtillus and Prunus spinosa.

Also sustains: Silver Washed Fritillary Argynnis paphia, Black-veined White Aporia crataegi, Lobster Moth Stauropus fagi, Coxcomb Prominent Lophopteryx capucina / camelina, Scarce Vapourer Orgyia recens / gonostigma, Dark Tussock Dasychira fascelina, Brown Tail Euproctis chrysorrhoea, Pale Eggar Trichiura crataegii, December Moth Poecilo campapopuli, Small Eggar Eriogaster lanestris, Oak Eggar Lasiocampa quercus, Lappet Gastropacha quercifolia, Chinese Character Cilix glaucata / spinula, Short-Cloaked Nola cucullatella, Dotted Clay Amathes baia, Least Yellow Underwing Triphaena interjecta, Gothic

Phalaena typica, Pale-shouldered Brocade Hadena thalassina, Small Quaker Orthosia cruda / pulverulenta, Clouded Drab Orthosia incerta / instabilis, Sprawler Brachyonycha sphinx / cassinia, Minor Shoulder-knot Bombycia viminalis, Golden-rod Brindle Lithomoia solidaginis, Green-Brindled Crescent Allophyes oxyacanthae, Dark Brocade Eumichtis adusta, Yellow-Line Quaker Agrochola macilenta, Flounced Chestnut Anchocelis helvola / rufina, Dark Chestnut Conistra ligula / spadicea, Dark Dagger Apatele tridens, Knotgrass moth Apatele rumicis, Mouse Amphipyra tragopogonis, Lunar-Spotted Pinion Cosmia pyralina, Nut-tree Tussock Colocasia coryli, Sussex Emerald Thalera fimbrialis, Little Emerald Iodis lactaearia, Common Marbled Carpet Dysstroma truncata / russata/ centumnotata, Mottled Pug Eupithecia exiguata, Common Pug Eupithecia vulgata, Autumnal Moth Oporinia autumnata, November Moth Oporinia dilutata / nebulata, August Thorn ennomos quercinaria / angularia, Brimstone Moth Opisthograptis luteolata / crataegata, Scarce Umber Eriannis aurantiara, Hedge Dagger Acronycta psi, Small Brindled Beauty Apocheima hispidaria, occasionally Blossom Underwing Orthosia miniosa.

Sustains in spring or after hibernation: Double Dart Graphiphora augur, Ingrailed Clay Diarsia festiva / primulae, Triple-spotted Clay Amathes ditrapezium, Square-spot Rustic Amathes xanthographa, Silvery Arches Polia hepatica / tincta, Double Square-spot Amathes triangulum, Lesser Yellow Underwing Triphaena comes / orbona, Lesser Broad-border Triphaena lanthina, Broad-bordered Yellow Underwing Lampra fimbriata / fimbria, Grey Arches Polia nebulosa, Old Lady Mormo maura, Figure of Eight Episema caeruleocephala, Common Emerald Hemithea aestivaria / strigata / thymiaria, V Pug Chloroclystis coronata (eats flowers), Double-striped Pug Gymnoscelis pumilata (eats flowers), and Deep Brown Dart Aporophyla lutulenta (unexpanded leaf buds).

Suffers: Hebrew Character Orthosia gothica, Gipsy Moth Lymantria dispar, Yellow / Gold Tail Euproctis similes / auriflua, Emperor Saturnia pavonia / carpini, Beautiful Arches Eumichtus satura, Grey Chi moth Antitype chi, and Grey Dagger Apatele psi.

CREPIS CAPILLARIS, SMOOTH HAWKSBEARD

Sustains: Shears Hada nana / dentina, Shark Cucullia umbratica, Small Ranunculus Hadena dysodea / chrysozona (flowers and seeds), Broad-barred White Hadena serena (flowers and seeds), and Marbled Clover Heliothis dipsacea /viriplaca (flowers and seeds).

CREPIS TARAXACIFOLIA, BEAKED HAWKSBEARD

Sustains: Autumnal Rustic Amathes glareosa, Yellow Belle Aspitates chrearia / citraria, and Shaded Pug Eupithecia subumbrata / scabiosata (eats flowers).

CUCURBITA PEPO, MARROW / ZUCCHINNI / COURGETTE / SUMMER SQUASH

Sustains / suffers Scarce Bordered Straw Heliothis armigera (eats immature fruits).

CUTWORMS & GROUND CATERPILLARS

These eat roots and cut off seedlings at ground level. Cut-worms are dingy brown, dirty grey with blackish spots. Yellowish greenish grey grubs with black or greenish stripes are soil living caterpillars Euxoa segetum, E. exclamationis and Graphiphora pronuba, which will decimate young seedlings and small plants. These all do most damage from mid to late summer and on into autumn and survive in pupal form from late winter into spring. As these are nocturnal they are easiest spotted with a torch on the surface at night. Causing similar damage are Swift moth Hepialus lupulinus root eating caterpillar grubs. Whitish with a red head these look similar to vine weevil grubs and may be found eating almost any herbaceous or bulbous plant roots.

CYMBALARIA MURALIS, IVY-LEAVED TOADFLAX

Sustains larvae of Feathered Ranunculus Eumichtis lichenea.

CYNOGLOSSUM OFFICINALE, HOUND'S-TONGUE

Flowers are rich in nectar.

Sustains: Scarlet Tiger Panaxia dominula, Coast Dart Euoxa cursoria, Flame Axylia putris, and Feathered Ranunculus Eumichtis lichenea.

CYPERUS LONGUS, GALINGALE

Sustains Rosy Rustic Hydraecia micacea.

CYTISUS SEE SAROTHAMNUS

DACTYLIS GLOMERATA, COCK'S-FOOT GRASS

Sustains 23 Lepidoptera larva.

<u>Sole sustainer of 3</u>: Tawny / Marbled Minor Procus latruncula (inside stems), Bordered Gothic Heliophobus anceps / saponariae / reticulata, and Rufous Minor Procus versicolour (inside stems).

<u>One of two sustainers of 2</u>: L-album Wainscot Leucania l-album other being Fescue, and Marbled Minor Procus strigilis (inside stems) other being Agropyron.

<u>One of three sustainers of 2</u>: Shoulder-striped Wainscot Leucania comma others being Rumex species, and Dark Arches Apamea monoglypha / polyodon others being Agropyron repens and Poa annua.

Also sustains: Clouded Brindle Apamea characterea / hepatica, Speckled Wood / Wood Argus Pararge negeria, Wall butterfly Pararge megera, Marbled White Melanargia galathea, Hedge Brown / Gatekeeper Maniola tithonus, Large Skipper Ochlodes venata / sylvanus, Ringlet Aphantopus hyperantus, Drinker Philudoria potatoria, Lunar Yellow Underwing Triphaena orbona / subsequa, Feathered Ear Pachetra sagittigera / leucophaea, Common Wainscott Leucania pallens, Smoky Wainscot Leucania impure, Double Line Mythimna turca, Common Rustic Apamea secalis / oculea / didyma (inside stems), Rosy Minor Procus literosa (inside stems), and Dusky Sallow Eremobia ochroleuca (seeds).

DAHLIA SPECIES

Occasionally, oddly, sustain Golden Rod Pug Eupithecia virgaureata (eats flowers) others usually being Quercus species, Senecio jacobea and Solidago.

Suffers: Mamestra brassicae Cabbage moth, Angle Shades moths Phlogophora meticulosa, and the tubers damaged by root eating white caterpillars of Swift moth Hepialus lupulinus.

DALDINIA CONCENTRICA, SHINING BLACK BRACKET FUNGUS

Sustains Waved Black Parascotia fuliginaria.

DAPHNE LAUREOLA

Greenish white evening flowers visited by night flying moths.

DATURA SPECIES, THORNAPPLES / ANGELS TRUMPETS

Sustains Bordered Straw Heliothis peltigera (mostly eats flowers and seeds).

DAUCUS CAROTA, CARROT

Wild and cultivated, left to bloom carrot flowers are rich in nectar and are recorded as visited by 61 species of insect: 2 butterflies and moths, 8 species bee, 19 species flies and 32 others.

Sustains 8 Lepidoptera larva: Swallow-tail Papilio machaon, Ground Lackey Malacosoma castrensis, Marbled Clover Heliothis dipsacea / viriplaca (flowers and seeds), Red Twin-spot Carpet Xanthorhoe spadicearia / ferrugata, and Yellow Belle Aspitates chrearia / citraria.

Also sustains / suffers: Common Flat-Body Moth Depressaria cicutella, and the seeds by Purple Carrot-seed Moth D. depressella, both of which are themselves predated by Odyneri species Solitary wasps. The carrot flowers and seeds also suffer Carrot-blossom Moth D. daucella, which may be lured onto parsnips which they apparently prefer.

DELPHINIUM AJACIS, LARKSPUR

Sole UK sustainer of Pease Blossom Periphanes delphinii (flowers and seeds).

Also sustains: Golden Plusia Polychrisia moneta (on seed pod first), and Swift moth Hepialus lupulinus white caterpillars (on roots).

DIAGRAPHIS ARUNDINACEA, REED-GRASS

Sustains Lunar Yellow Underwing Triphaena orbona / subsequa.

DIANTHUS ARMERIA, DEPTFORD PINK

Sustains Mullein Wave Scopula marginepunctata / promutata / incanata.

Suffer Carnation Tortrix moths Tortrix pronubana which roll leaves together, may also enter flowerbuds to eat out the middle.

DIANTHUS BARBATUS, SWEET WILLIAM

Sustains Tawny Shears Hadena lepida / carpophaga (mostly on seeds).

Suffer Carnation Tortrix moths Tortrix pronubana which roll leaves together, may also enter flowerbuds to eat out the middle.

DIGITALIS PURPUREA, FOXGLOVE

Sole sustainer of Foxglove Pug Eupithecia pulchellata moth (eats flowers).

Also sustains: Heath Fritillary Melitaea athalia, Lesser Yellow Underwing Triphaena comes / orbona, and Small Angle-Shades Euplexia lucipara. Suffers unspecified caterpillars that bore down stems causing wilting.

DIGRAPHIS ARUNDINACEA, REED GRASS

One of two sustainers of 2: Small Clouded Brindle (sic) other being Phalaris, and Double Lobed Apamea ophiogramma (in stems) other being Phalaris.

Also sustains: Drinker Philudoria potatoria, Southern Wainscot Leucania straminea, and Dusky Brocade Apamea obscura / gemina / remissa.

DIPSACUS FULLONUM, TEASELS

Importantly leaf joints hold water droplets for insects to drink.

Sustains Mottled Rustic Caradrina morpheus.

Dryas octopetala, WHITE DRYAS

Sustains Emperor Saturnia pavonia / carpini.

DUN-BAR moth Cosmia trapezina

Eats foliage of many trees but later larval instars most interestingly consume larvae of other Lepidoptera.

Echinops ritro, GLOBE THISTLE

Flowers rich in nectar.

One of two sustainers Purple Marbled Eublemma ostrina other being Carlina vulgaris.

Echium vulgare, VIPER'S BUGLOSS

Flowers rich in nectar.

Sustains: Painted Lady Vanessa cardui, and Crimson-speckled Utetheisa pulchella.

Elymus arenarius, LYME GRASS

Sole sustainer of Lyme Grass Arenostola elymi (in stems).

Empetrum nigrum, CROWBERRY

Sole sustainer of Black Mountain-moth Psodos coracina / trepidata.

One of three sustainers of 2: Northern Dart Amathes alpicola / hyperborea / alpina others being Arctostaphylos and Vaccinium myrtillus, and Weaver's Wave Sterrha churnata / contiguaria others being Calluna vulgaris and Cotyledon.

Also sustains: Green Hairstreak Callophrys rubi, (blossoms and leaves), Autumnal Rustic Amathes glareosa, and Grey Mountain Carpet Entephria caesiata.

Epilobium angustifolium, ROSE BAY WILLOW-HERB

One of three sustainers Small Phoenix Ecliptopera silaceata others being Circaea and E. montanum.

Also sustains: Bedstraw Hawkmoth Celerio / Deilephila galii, Elephant Hawkmoth Deilephila / Chaerocampa elpenor, Small Elephant Hawkmoth Deilephila porcellus, Brown Line Lucania / Leucania conigera.

Suffers Setaceous Hebrew Character Amathes e-nigrum.

Epilobium hirsutum, HAIRY WILLOW-HERB

Tallest of genus and one most often seen then commonly misidentified as the Rose Bay.

Sustains: Small Elephant Hawkmoth Deilephila porcellus, Elephant Hawkmoth Deilephila / Chaerocampa elpenor, Silver Striped Hawkmoth Hippotion celerio, and Gothic Phalaena typica (after hibernation).

Suffers Setaceous Hebrew Character Amathes e-nigrum.

Epilobium montanum, BROAD-LEAVED WILLOW-HERB

One of two sustainers White-Banded Carpet Euphyia luctuata other being Galium species.

One of three sustainers Small Phoenix Ecliptopera silaceata others being Circaea and E. angustifolum.

Suffers Setaceous Hebrew Character Amathes e-nigrum.

Epilobium palustre, MARSH WILLOW-HERB

Sustains Elephant Hawkmoth Deilephila elpenor.

Suffers Setaceous Hebrew Character Amathes e-nigrum.

Epilobium tetragonum, SQUARE-STEMMED WILLOW HERB

Sustains Black Rustic Aporophyla nigra.

Suffers Setaceous Hebrew Character Amathes e-nigrum.

Equisetum arvense, HORSETAIL, OFTEN WRONGLY CALLED MARESTAIL

Sustains Rosy Rustic Hydraecia micacea.

Erica cinerea, BELL HEATHER

Sustains 27 Lepidoptera larva.

One of two sustainers of 2: True Lover's Knot Lycophotia varia / porphyrea / strigula other being Calluna species, and Beautiful Yellow Underwing Anarta myrtilli other being Calluna species.

One of three sustainers of 5: Neglected / Grey Rustic Amathes castanea / neglecta others being Salix atrocinerea and Salix caprea, Cousin German Triphaena sobrina others being Betula and Vaccinium myrtillus, Heath Rustic Amathes agathina others being Calluna vulgaris and Erica tetralix, Beautiful Snout Bomolocha crassalis / fontis others being Erica tetralix and Vaccinium myrtillus, and Scalloped Bar Dyscia fagaria others being Calluna vulgaris and Erica tetralix.

Also sustains: Silver-Studded Blue Phlebius argus / aegon, Pale Eggar Trichiura crataegii, Ashworth's Rustic Amathes ashworthii, Autumnal Rustic Amathes glareosa, Glaucous Shears Hadena bombycina / glauca, Fox Moth Macrothylacia rubi, Emperor Saturnia pavonia / carpini, Speckled Footman Coscinia cribraria / cribrum, Dark Brocade Eumichtis adusta, Grey Mountain Carpet Entephria caesiata, Ling Pug Eupithecia goossensiata / minutata (flowers and seeds), Rannoch Brindled Beauty Poccilopsis lapponaria, Ringed Carpet Cleora cinctaria, Scotch Annulet Gnophos myrtillata / obfuscaria, Common Heath-moth Ematurga atomaria, Grey Grass Wave Perconia strigillaria, Buff Tiger Nemeophila russula, Ruby Tiger Spilosoma / Phragmatobia fuliginosa, Oak Eggar Bombyx / Lasiocampa quercus, and Ingrailed / Engrailed Clay Noctua Diarsia festiva / primulae.

Erica tetralix, CROSS-LEAVED HEATH

Sustains 15 Lepidoptera larva.

One of three sustainers of 3: Beautiful Snout Bomolocha crassalis / fontis others being E. cinerea and Vaccinium myrtillus, Heath Rustic Amathes agathina others being Calluna vulgaris and E. cinerea, and Grey Scalloped Bar Dyscia fagaria others being Calluna vulgaris and E. cinerea.

Also sustains: Fox Moth Macrothylacia rubi, Emperor Saturnia pavonia / carpini, Speckled Footman Coscinia cribraria / cribrum, Dark Brocade Eumichtis adusta, Small Grass Emerald Chlorissa viridata, Grey Mountain Carpet Entephria caesiata, Rannoch Brindled Beauty Poccilopsis lapponaria, Ringed Carpet Cleora cinctaria, Scotch Annulet Gnophos myrtillata / obfuscaria, Buff Tiger Nemeophila russula, Ling Pug Eupithecia goossensiata / minutata (flowers and seeds), and Green Hairstreak Callophrys rubi (foliage and flowers).

Eriophorum angustifolium / polystachion, COMMON COTTON-GRASS

<u>One of two sustainers</u> Haworth's Minor (inside stems) other being E. vaginatum.

Also sustains: Large Heath / Marsh Ringlet butterfly Coenonympha tullia / davus / tiphon, and Small Wainscot Arenostola pygmina / fulva (in flower stem).

Eriophorum vaginatum, HARE'S-TAIL COTTON-GRASS

<u>One of two sustainers</u> Haworth's Minor Celaena haworthii (in stems) other E. angustifolium.

Also sustains Antler Cerapteryx graminis.

Erodium cicutarium, HEMLOCK STORK'S-BILL

<u>One of two sustainers</u> Brown Argus Aricia agestis / astrarche / artaxerxes/ medon / salmacis other being Helianthemum.

Also sustains Bordered Straw Heliothis peltigera (mostly eats flowers and seeds).

Eryngium maritimum, SEA HOLLY

Flowers rich in nectar.

Sustains Sand Dart Agrotis ripae.

ERYSIUM CHEIRANTHOIDES, TREACLE MUSTARD

One of two sustainers Grey Carpet Lithostege griseata / nivearia (seed pods) other being Sisymbrium.

Also sustains Bath White Pontia daplidice.

ERYTHRAEA CENTAURIUM, CENTAURY

Contains no discernible nectar yet oddly is frequently visited by butterflies.

EUONYMOUS EUROPAEUS, SPINDLE

Sole sustainer of Scorched Carpet Ligdia adustata.

Also sustains: Death's-head Hawkmoth Acherontia atropos, and Holly / Azure Blue Celastrina argiolus (flowers, flower buds, green berries and leaves).

EUONYMOUS JAPONICUS, GARDEN FORMS

Sustain Magpie Abraxas grossulariata.

EUPATORIUM CANNABINUM, HEMP AGRIMONY

Flowers rich in nectar observed visited by 18 different insect species: 9 butterflies and moths, 2 species bee, 6 species flies and 1 other.

Sustains 8 Lepidoptera larva.

Sole sustainer of Scarce Burnished Brass Plusia chryson / orichalcea.

Also sustains: Kent Black-Arches Nola albula / albulalis, Wormwood Pug Eupithecia absinthiata / minutata, Gold Spangle Plusia bractea, Gem moth Nycterosea obstipata / fluviata / gemmata, Frosted Orange Gortyna flavago /ochracea (in stems), Lime-speck Pug Eupithecia centaureata / oblongata (flowers), and V Pug Chloroclystis coronata (flowers).

Euphorbia amygdaloides WOOD SPURGE

One of three sustainers Drab Looper Minoa murinata / euphorbiata others being E. peplus and E. cyparissius.

Also sustains Double Square-spot Amathes triangulum.

Euphorbia cyparissius, CYPRESS SPURGE

One of three sustainers Drab Looper Minoa murinata / euphorbiata others being E. peplus and E. amygdaloides.

Also sustains Spurge Hawkmoth Celerio / Deilephila euphorbiae,

Euphorbia paralias, SEA SPURGE

Sole sustainers of larvae of Spurge Hawkmoth Celerio euphorbiae.

Also sustains Coast Dart Euoxa cursoria.

Euphorbia segetalis portlandica, PORTLAND SPURGE

Sole sustainers of larvae of Spurge Hawkmoth Celerio euphorbiae.

Also sustains Coast Dart Euoxa cursoria.

Euphorbia peplus, PETTY SPURGE

<u>One of two sustainers</u> Drab Looper Minoa murinata /
euphorbiata others being E. amygdaloides and E. cyparissius.

Euphrasia officinalis, EYEBRIGHT

<u>Sole sustainer of 2</u>: Pretty Pinion Perizoma blandiata /
adaequata (in seed capsules), and Heath Rivulet Perizoma
minorata / ericetata (in seed capsules).

<u>One of two sustainers</u> Barred Rivulet Perizoma bifaciata /
unifasciata (in seed capsules) other being Bartsia.

Fagopyrum esculentum, BUCKWHEAT

Sustain / suffer White-line Dart Euoxa tritici / aquilina (mostly on young plants).

Fagus sylvatica, BEECH

Sustains 28 Lepidoptera larva.

<u>Sole sustainer of 2</u>: Barred Hook-Tip Drepana cultraria / unguicula, and Clay Triple-lines Cosymbia linearia / trilinearia.

<u>One of two sustainers</u> Marbled Pug Eupithecia irriguata other being Quercus species.

<u>One of three sustainers</u> Clouded Magpie Abraxas sylvata / ulmata others being Corylus and Ulmus.

Also sustains: Northern Winter Moth Operophtera fagata / boreata, Lobster Moth Stauropus fagi, Coxcomb Prominent Lophopteryx capucina / camelina, Scarce Vapourer Orgyia recens / gonostigma, Black V moth Leucoma v-nigrum / l-album, Least Black Arches Celama confusalis / cristulalis, Broad-bordered Yellow Underwing Lampra fimbriata / fimbria. (after hibernation), Common Quaker Orthosia stabilis, Sprawler Brachyonycha sphinx / cassinia, Satellite Eupsilia transversa / satellitia, Yellow-Line Quaker Agrochola macilenta, Barred Sallow Tiliacea aurago, Green Silver-Lines Bena fagana / prasinana, Nut-tree Tussock Colocasia coryli, Large Emerald Geometra papilionaria, Pale November Moth Oporinia christyi, August Thorn Ennomos quercinaria / angularia, September

Thorn Deuteronomos erosaria, Scorched Wing Plagodis dolobraria, Square-Spot Ectropis consonaria, and occasionally Marbled Brown Drymonia dodonaea / trimacula.

Suffers: Buff-Tip Phalera bucephala, and Yellow / Gold Tail Euproctis similes / auriflua.

FERNS
As with many flowering plants these sustain / suffer the Broom moth Ceramica pisi.

Festuca arenaria, SEA FESCUE-GRASS
Sustains Portland Moth Actebia praecox, and Wall butterfly Pararge megera.

Festuca elatior, MEADOW FESCUE-GRASS
Sole sustainer of Bond's Wainscot Arenostola morrisii / bondii.

One of two sustainers L-album Wainscot Leucania l-album other being Dactylis.

One of three sustainers Cloaked Minor Procus furuncula / bicoloria (in stems) others being Aira caespitosa and Arrhenatherum elatius.

Also sustains: Common Rustic Apamea secalis / oculea / didyma (in stems), and Wall butterfly Pararge megera.

Festuca ovina, SHEEP'S FESCUE-GRASS
Sustains 8 Lepidoptera larva.

Sole sustainer of Silver-spotted Skipper Hesperia comma.

Sustains: Marbled White Melanargia galathea, Grayling Satyrus semele, Feathered Footman Coscinia striata / grammica, Northern Rustic Ammogrotis lucernea, Large Heath / Marsh Ringlet butterfly Coenonympha tullia / davus / tiphon, Common Rustic Apamea secalis / oculea / didyma (in stems), and Wall butterfly Pararge megera.

Festuca pratensis MEADOW FESCUE-GRASS

Sustains: Large Heath / Marsh Ringlet butterfly Coenonympha tullia / davus / tiphon, and Wall butterfly Pararge megera.

Filago germanica, COMMON CUDWEED

Sustains Painted Lady Vanessa cardui.

Filipendula / Spiraea ulmaria, MEADOWSWEET

Sustains 9 Lepidoptera larva.

Sole sustainer of Marsh-Moth Hydrillula palustris.

One of two sustainers Lesser Cream Wave Scopula immutata other being Valeriana.

Also sustains: Buff Arches Habrosyne pyritoides / derasa, Scarlet Tiger Panaxia dominula, Powdered Quaker Orthosia gracilis, Brown-Spot Pinion Anchocelis litura, Sweet-Gale Apatele euphorbiae / myricae, Mullein Wave Scopula marginepunctata / promutata / incanata, and Rosy Rustic Hydraecia micacea (in roots).

FOENICULUM VULGARE, FENNEL

Sustains: Swallow-tail Papilio machaon, and Mouse Amphipyra tragopogonis.

FORSYTHIA SPECIES

Sustains Privet Hawkmoth Sphinx ligustri.

FRAGARIA SPECIES, STRAWBERRIES

Sustain 15 Lepidoptera larvae: Dingy Skipper Erynns tages, Grizzled Skipper Pyrgus malvae / alveolus, Fox Moth Macrothylacia rubi, Kent Black-Arches Nola albula / albulalis, Six-striped Rustic Amathes sexstrigata / umbrosa, Orange Wainscot / Brown-line Bright-eye Leucania conigera, Knotgrass moth Apatele rumicis, Mouse Amphipyra tragopogonis, Beautiful Carpet Mesoleuca albicillata, Yellow Shell Euphyia bilineata, Common Marbled Carpet Dysstroma truncata / russata/ centumnotata, Dark Marbled Carpet Dysstroma citrata / immanata, and Annulet Gnophos obscurata / pullata. Also sustain / suffer Leaf Button / Strawberry moth Peronea conariana larvae, greenish with yellow head, hatches in late spring eating and webbing together blossom buds and leaves, often living in a web on the underside of leaves. Strawberries also suffer Small / Garden Swift moth Hepialus lupulinus eating their roots.

Fraxinus excelsior, ASH

With one of the briefest canopy periods of UK trees, coming into leaf late and falling early it's foliage still sustains 18 different Lepidoptera larva.

Sole sustainer of 4: Tawny Pinion Lithophane semibrunnea, Centre-Barred Sallow Atethmia xerampelina, Ash Pug Eupithecia innotata / fraxinata (though occasionally on Artemesias), and Dusky Thorn Deuteronomos fuscantaria.

One of two sustainers White Letter Hairstreak Strymonidia w-album other being Ulmus species.

Also sustains: Privet Hawkmoth Sphinx ligustri, December Moth Poecilo campapopuli, Sprawler Brachyonycha sphinx / cassinia, Pale Pinion Lithophane socia / petrificata, Coronet Craniophora ligustri, Copper Underwing Amphipyra pyramidea, Red-green Carpet Chloroclysta siterata / psittacata, Mottled Pug Eupithecia exiguata, Lunar Thorn Selenia lunaria, Little Thorn Cepphis advenaria, Flame Brocade Trigonophora flammea / empyrea (last instar on young buds), Brick Agrochola circellaris / ferruginea (flowers and seeds), and Goat Moth Cossus ligniperda (wood live and dead).

Fuchsia

Sustain: Silver Striped Hawkmoth Hippotion celerio, Striped Hawkmoth Celerio livornica, occasionally sustains Elephant Hawkmoth Deilephila elpenor.

GALEOPSIS LADANUM, RED HEMP-NETTLE

<u>One of two sustainers</u> Small Rivulet Perizoma alchemillata / rivulata (seeds) other being Stachys.

Sustains Satyr Pug Eupithecia satyrata (eats flowers).

GALEOPSIS TETRAHIT, COMMON HEMP-NETTLE

<u>One of two sustainers</u> Small Rivulet Perizoma alchemillata / rivulata (seeds) other being Stachys.

Also sustains: Burnished Brass Plusia chrysitis, and Satyr Pug Eupithecia satyrata (eats flowers).

GALIUM APARINE, GOOSE-GRASS / CLEAVERS / STICKY WEED

Sustains 6 Lepidoptera larva.

<u>Sole sustainers of 3:</u> Mottled Grey Colostygia multistrigaria are Galium species, Water Carpet Lampropteryx suffumata other Galium species, Devon Carpet Lampropteryx otregiata other Galium species

<u>One of two sustainers:</u> White-Banded Carpet Euphyia luctuata other being Epilobium.

Also sustains: Gothic Phalaena typica (after hibernation), Barred Straw Lygris pyraliata / dotata.

GALIUM MOLLUGO, HEDGE BEDSTRAW

Sustains 31 Lepidoptera larvae.

Sole sustainers of 6: Single-dotted Beech-green Carpet Colostygia pectinataria / viridaria (sic, seems conflated with Green Carpet below), Beech-green Carpet Colostygia olivata other Galium species, Common Carpet Epirrhoe alternata / sociata / subtristata other Galium species, Wood Carpet Epirrhoe rivata other Galium species, Water Carpet Lampropteryx suffumata other Galium species, Royal Mantle Euphyia cuculata / sinuate (flowers) other Galium species, and Flame Euphyia rubidata other being Galium species.

One of three sustainers of 5: Single dotted / Wave Sterrha dimidiata / scutulata (flowers and leaves) others being Anthriscus and Pimpinella, Hummingbird Hawkmoth Macroglossum stellatarum others being other Galium species and Rubia, Striped Twin-spot Carpet Colostygia salicata others being other Galium species, likewise Purple Bar Lyncometra ocellata others all being other Galium species, and also Galium Carpet Epirrhoe galiata others all being other Galium species.

Also sustains: Cream Wave Scopula floslactata / remutata / remutaria, White-line Dart Euoxa tritici / aquilina, Archer's Dart Agrotis vestigialis / valligera, Six-striped Rustic Amathes sexstrigata / umbrosa, Flame Axylia putris, Bedstraw Hawkmoth Celerio / Deilephila galii, Small Elephant Hawkmoth Deilephila / Chaerocampa porcellus, Mottled Rustic Caradrina morpheus, Small Scallop Sterrha emarginata, Plain Wave Sterrha inornata, Large Twin-spot Carpet Xanthorhoe quadrifasiata, Dark-barred Twin-spot Carpet Xanthorhoe ferrugata / unidentaria, Red Twin-spot Carpet Xanthorhoe spadicearia / ferrugata, Silver-ground Carpet Xanthorhoe montanata, Oblique Carpet Orthonama lignata / vittata, and sustains Green Carpet Colostygia pectinataria / viridaria, Barred Straw Lygris pyraliata / dotata, and Satyr Pug Eupithecia satyrata (eats flowers).

GALIUM PALUSTRE, MARSH BEDSTRAW

Sustains 10 Lepidoptera larva.

Sole sustainer of Many-lined Euphyia polygrammata.

Also sustains: Elephant Hawkmoth Deilephila / Chaerocampa elpenor, Autumnal Rustic Amathes glareosa, Red Chestnut Cerastis rubricosa, Cream Wave Scopula floslactata / remutata / remutaria, Dark-barred Twin-spot Carpet Xanthorhoe ferrugata / unidentaria, Oblique Carpet Orthonama lignata / vittata, Satyr Pug Eupithecia satyrata (eats flowers). Red-headed Chestnut Conistra erythrocephala feeds first on oak then on Galiums when underneath.

GALIUM SAXATILE, HEATH BEDSTRAW

Sustains 16 Lepidoptera larva.

Sole sustainer of Small Argent & Sable Epirrhoe tristata.

Possible other sustainer Devon Carpet Lampropteryx otregiata see Galium above.

One of three sustainers of 5: Mottled Grey Colostygia multistrigaria is only sustained by other Galium species, as is Striped Twin-spot Carpet Colostygia salicata others being other Galium species, likewise Purple Bar Lyncometra ocellata others being other Galium species, and Galium Carpet Epirrhoe galiata others being other Galium species.

Also sustains: Bedstraw Hawkmoth Celerio / Deilephila galii, Small Elephant Hawkmoth Deilephila / Chaerocampa porcellus, Plain Wave Sterrha inornata, Cream Wave Scopula floslactata / remutata / remutaria, Large Twin-spot Carpet Xanthorhoe quadrifasiata, Dark-barred Twin-spot Carpet Xanthorhoe ferrugata / unidentaria, Oblique Carpet Orthonama lignata /

vittata, Green Carpet Colostygia pectinataria / viridaria, and Satyr Pug Eupithecia satyrata (eats flowers),

GALIUM VERUM, LADY'S BEDSTRAW

Sustains 32 Lepidoptera larva.

<u>Sole sustainer of</u> Oblique-striped Mesotype virgata / lineolata.

<u>One of two sustainers</u> <u>of 6</u>: Square-spot Dart Euoxa obelisca other being Helianthemum, Wood Carpet Epirrhoe rivata other Galium species, Beech-green Carpet Colostygia olivata other Galium species, Common Carpet Epirrhoe alternata / sociata / subtristata other Galium species, Royal Mantle Euphyia cuculata / sinuate (eats flowers) other Galium species, Flame Euphyia rubidata other Galium species.

<u>One of three sustainers:</u> Hawkmoth Macroglossum stellatarum others being Galium species and Rubia, Mottled Grey Colostygia multistrigaria is only sustained by other Galium species, as is Striped Twin-spot Carpet Colostygia salicata others all being other Galium species, and Purple Bar Lyncometra ocellata others all being other Galium species, and Galium Carpet Epirrhoe galiata others all being other Galium species.

Also sustains: Barred Straw Lygris pyraliata / dotata, Hummingbird Striped Hawkmoth Celerio livornica, Silver Striped Hawkmoth Hippotion celerio, Flame Shoulder Ochropleura plect, Ashworth's Rustic Amathes ashworthii, White-line Dart Euoxa tritici / aquilina, Archer's Dart Agrotis vestigialis / valligera, Six-striped Rustic Amathes sexstrigata / umbrosa, Flame Axylia putris, Bedstraw Hawkmoth Celerio galli, Small Elephant Hawkmoth Deilephila / Chaerocampa porcellus, Small Scallop Sterrha emarginata, Plain Wave Sterrha inornata, Riband Wave Sterrha aversata, Cream Wave Scopula floslactata /

remutata / remutaria, Large Twin-spot Carpet Xanthorhoe quadrifasiata, Dark-barred Twin-spot Carpet Xanthorhoe ferrugata / unidentaria, Red Twin-spot Carpet Xanthorhoe spadicearia / ferrugata, Oblique Carpet Orthonama lignata / vittata, Satyr Pug Eupithecia satyrata (eats flowers).

Galium uliginosum SWAMP BEDSTRAW

Sustains 9 Lepidoptera larvae: Elephant Hawkmoth Deilephila / Chaerocampa elpenor, Autumnal Rustic Amathes glareosa, Red Chestnut Cerastis rubricosa, Plain Wave Sterrha inornata, Cream Wave Scopula floslactata / remutata / remutaria, Large Twin-spot Carpet Xanthorhoe quadrifasiata, and Satyr Pug Eupithecia satyrata (eats flowers). The Red-headed Chestnut Conistra erythrocephala feeds on oak first but later on Galiums when any underneath.

Genista anglica NEEDLE-FURZE

Sustain 8 Lepidoptera larva.

One of three sustainers Grass Emerald Pseudoterpna pruinata / cytisaria others being Sarothamnus and Ulex.

Also sustains: Silver-Studded Blue Phlebius argus / aegon, Green Hairstreak Callophrys rubi (flowers and leaves), Small Grass Emerald Chlorissa viridata, Little Emerald Iodis lactaearia, Lead Belle Ortholitha mucronata / plumbaria / palumbaria, Scotch Annulet Gnophos myrtillata / obfuscaria, and Black-veined Moth Siona lineata / dealbata.

Genista tinctoria, DYER'S GREENWEED

Sustains 6 Lepidoptera larvae: Light Brocade Hadena w-latinum / genistae, Powdered Quaker Orthosia gracilis, Northern Drab

Orthosia advena / opima (flowers), Green Hairstreak Callophrys rubi (flowers and leaves), Scotch Annulet Gnophos myrtillata / obfuscaria, and Black-veined Moth Siona lineata / dealbata.

Gentiana amarelle, AUTUMN GENTIAN
Sustain Shaded Pug Eupithecia subumbrata / scabiosata (flowers).

Gentiana campestris, FIELD GENTIAN
Sustain Shaded Pug Eupithecia subumbrata / scabiosata (flowers).

Geranium lucidium, SHINING CRANE'S-BILL
Sustains: Annulet Gnophos obscurata / pullata, and Swallow-tailed moth Ourapteryx sambucaria.

Suffers: Angle Shades Moth Phogophora meticulosa, and Cabbage moth Mamestra brassicae.

Geranium sanguineum, BLOODY CRANE'S-BILL
Sustains: Fox Moth Macrothylacia rubi, Swallow-tailed moth Ourapteryx sambucaria, and Annulet Gnophos obscurata / pullata.

Suffers: Angle Shades Moth Phogophora meticulosa, and Cabbage moth Mamestra brassicae.

Geum rivale, WATER AVENS
Often found as hybrid with G. urbanum.

Sustains Riband Wave Sterrha aversata.

GEUM URBANUM, WOOD AVENS
Often found as hybrid with G. rivale.

Sustains: Beautiful Golden Y Plusia pulchrina, and Riband Wave Sterrha aversata.

GLADIOLI
Suffers: Yellow / Gold Tail Euproctis similes / auriflua, Scarce Bordered Straw Heliothis armigera, Swift moth grubs on the roots causing flagging plants and holed corms, and Angle Shades moth Phogophora meticulosa with green or olive brown caterpillars feeding on leaves, flowerbuds and blooms.

GLAUX MARITIME, SEA MILKWORT
Sustains Sand Dart Agrotis ripae.

GLECHOMA HEDERACEA, GROUND IVY
<u>One of three sustainers</u> Pale shoulder Tarache solaris / lucida others being Convolvulus and Malva.

Also sustains: Gold Spangle Plusia bractea, Mullein Wave Scopula marginepunctata / promutata / incanata, Dark-barred Twin-spot Carpet Xanthorhoe ferrugata / unidentaria, and Red Twin-spot Carpet Xanthorhoe spadicearia / ferrugata.

Gnaphalium arenarium, CUDWEED

<u>One of two sustainers</u> Scarce Marbled Eublemma noctualis / paula (eats flowers) other being Antennaria.

Godetia

Sustains Elephant Hawkmoth Deilephila / Chaerocampa elpenor.

Grasses

Sustain / suffer over 25 Lepidoptera larvae.

Sustain: White-speck Wainscot Leucania unipuncta, Delicate Wainscot Leucania vitellina, Cosmopolitan Leucania loreyi, Union Rusttic Apamea pabulatricula / connexa, Large Nutmeg Apamea infesta / anceps / sordida, Smoky Wainscot Leucania impura, Southern Wainscot Leucania straminea, Common Wainscot Leucania pallens, Shoulder-Knot Apamea basilinea, White Ear / Common Rustic Apamea didyma, Middle-Barred Minor Miana / Procus fascinuncula / fasciuncula, Anomalous Stilbia anomala, Hay Moth / Pale Mottled Willow Caradrina quadripunctata, Dark Swordgrass Agrotis suffusa / ipsilon, Heart and Dart Agrotis exclamationis, Double Dart Noctua / Graphiphora augur, Clouded Brindle Xylophasia rurea, Dark Arches Xylophasia monoglypha (on roots), Feathered Gothic Neuronia / Pachetra popularis (on roots), and Ear Moth Hydraecia nictitans (on roots).

Suffers: Silver Gamma / Y moth Plusia gamma, Antler / Grass Moth Cerapteryx / Charaeus graminis, Belted Beauty Nyssia zonaria, and Great Yellow Underwing moth Noctua / Tryphaena pronuba (roots and leaves).

HEDERA HELIX, IVY

Sustains 9 Lepidoptera larvae.

One of three sustainers of 2: Fanfoot Zanclognatha tarsipennalis others being Rubus idaeus and Salix caprea, and Treble Brown-spot Sterrha trigeminata / scutularia (flowers) others being Acer campestre and Hedera.

Also sustains: Swallow-tailed moth Ourapteryx sambucaria, Willow Beauty Alcis rhomboidaria / gemmaria, Small Dusty Wave Sterrha seriata /incanata / virgularia, Holly / Azure Blue Celastrina argiolus (eats flowers, flower buds, green berries and leaves) (in autumn), and Yellow-barred Brindle Acasis viretata (eats flowers first, then green berries then leaves).

Suffers: Magpie Abraxas grossulariata, and Dot Melanchra persicariae.

HELENIUM AMARUM, BITTER SNEEZEWEED

Flowers rich in nectar.

Sustains / suffers Tortix moth caterpillars Cephasia species which stick leaves together and hide inside.

HELIANTHEMUM NUMMULARIUM / CHAEMAECISTUS, ROCK-ROSE

Sustains 7 Lepidoptera larva.

Sole sustainer of Silky Wave Sterrha dilutaria / holosericeata (on withered leaves).

One of two sustainers of 2: Brown Argus Aricia agestis / astrarche / artaxerxes / medon / salmacis other being Erodium, and Square-spot Dart Euoxa obelisca other being Galium species.

Also sustains: Wood Tiger Parasemia plantaginis, Ashworth's Rustic Amathes ashworthii, Green Hairstreak Callophrys rubi (flowers and leaves), and Annulet Gnophos obscurata / pullata.

HELIOTROPIUM EUROPAEUM HYBRIDUM, HELIOTROPE
Tender garden plant deep blue flowers rich in nectar.

Sustains Crimson-speckled Utetheisa pulchella.

HERACLEUM SPHONDYLIUM, HOGWEED
Sole sustainer of Brindled Ochre Dasypolia templi (first flowers then stems).

One of three sustainers White-spotted Pug Eupithecia tripunctaria / albipunctata (eats flowers) others being Angelica and Pastinaca.

Also sustains: Swallow-tail Papilio machaon, Plain Golden Y Plusia iota, and Triple-spotted Pug Eupithecia trisignaria (flowers and seeds).

Suffers Garden Dart Euoxa nigricans.

Hesperis matronalis, DAME'S VIOLET / SWEET ROCKET

Sustains / suffers: Silver Washed Fritillary Argynnis paphia, Green-veined White Pieris napi, and Orange-Tip Anthocaris cardamines.

Hieracium murorum, WALL HAWKWEED

Sustains: Ashworth's Rustic Amathes ashworthii, and Marbled Clover Heliothis dipsacea / viriplaca (flowers and seeds).

Hieracium pilosella, MOUSE-EAR HAWKWEED

Sole sustainer of Feathered Footman Coscinia striata / grammica.

Also sustains: Clouded Buff Diacrisia sannio / russula, Shears Hada nana / dentina, Shark Cucullia umbratica, Gold Spangle Plusia bractea, Broad-barred White Hadena serena (flowers and seeds), and Marbled Clover Heliothis dipsacea / viriplaca (flowers and seeds).

Hippocrepis comosa, HORSESHOE VETCH

Sole sustainer of Clifden / Adonis Blue Lysandra bellargus / adonis.

Also sustains: Chalkhill Blue Lysandra coridon, Dingy Skipper Erynnis tages, Mullein Wave Scopula marginepunctata / promutata / incanata, and Chalk Carpet Ortholitha bipunctaria.

HIPPOPHAE RHAMNOIDES, SEA BUCKTHORN

Sustains Brown Tail Euproctis chrysorrhoea / phaecorrhoea.

HOLCUS LANATUS, MEADOW SOFT GRASS / YORKSHIRE FOG

<u>One of two sustainers</u> Lunar Underwing Omphaloscelis lunosa other being Poa.

Also sustains: Antler Cerapteryx graminis, Small Skipper Thymelicus sylvestris / linea / thaumus, and Large Skipper Ochlodes venata / sylvanus.

HOLCUS MOLLIS CREEPING SOFT-GRASS

Sustains: Large Skipper Ochlodes venata / sylvanus, and Common Rustic Apamea secalis / oculea / didyma (in stems).

HORDEUM DISTICHON / VULGARE, BARLEY

<u>One of three sustainers</u> Flounced Rustic Luperina testacea (on roots) others being Avena and Triticum.

Also sustains: Rosy Minor Procus literosa (in stems), Rosy Rustic Hydraecia micacea (in stems), and Brighton Wainscot Oria musculosa (in stems).

HUMULUS LUPULUS, HOPS

Sustains 16 Lepidoptera larva.

<u>Sole sustainer of</u> Buttoned Snout Hypena rostralis.

One of two sustainers of 3: Snout Hypena proboscidalis other being Urtica dioica, Dark Spectacle Abrostola triplasia / trigemina other being Urtica dioica, and Peacock Nymphalis / Inachis io other also being Urtica dioica.

One of three sustainers of 2: Currant Pug Eupithecia assimilata others being Ribes species, and Red Admiral Vanessa atalanta others being Parietaria and Urtica dioica.

Also sustains: Comma Polygonia c-album Pale Tussock Dasychira pudibunda, Cinnabar Callimorpha jacobaea, Clouded Drab Orthosia incerta / instabilis, Twin-Spotted Quaker Orthosia munda, Knotgrass moth Apatele rumicis, Mottled Rustic Caradrina morpheus, Rosy Rustic Hydraecia micacea, and occasionally Privet Hawkmoth Sphinx ligustri.

HYOSCYAMUS NIGER, HENBANE

Sustains: Scarce Bordered Straw Heliothis armigera, Bordered Sallow Pyrrhia umbra / marginata (flowers and seeds), and Bordered Straw Heliothis peltigera (mostly eats flowers and seeds).

HYPERICUM ELOIDES, MARSH ST JOHNS WORT

One of two sustainers Treble Bar Anaitis plagiata other being H. species.

One of three sustainers Lesser Treble Bar Anaitis efformata others being other Hypericums.

Also sustains: Satyr Pug Eupithecia satyrata (flowerbuds), Black-veined Moth Siona lineata / dealbata (flowers), and Powdered Quaker Orthosia gracilis.

HYPERICUM PERFORATUM, PERFORATED St. JOHN'S WORT

<u>Sole sustainer of</u> Purple Cloud Actinotia polyodon / perspicillaris.

<u>One of two sustainers</u>: Treble Bar Anaitis plagiata other H. species.

<u>One of three sustainers</u> Lesser Treble Bar Anaitis efformata others being other Hypericums.

Also sustains: Sussex Emerald Thalera fimbrialis, V Pug Chloroclystis coronata (flowers), Satyr Pug Eupithecia satyrata (flowerbuds), and Black-veined Moth Siona lineata / dealbata (flowers).

HYPERICUM PULCHRUM SLENDER St. JOHN'S WORT

<u>One of two sustainers</u> Treble Bar Anaitis plagiata other H. species.

<u>One of three sustainers</u> Lesser Treble Bar Anaitis efformata others being other Hypericums.

Also sustains: Satyr Pug Eupithecia satyrata (flowerbuds), and Black-veined Moth Siona lineata / dealbata (flowers).

IBERIS UMBELLATA, CANDYTUFT

Sustains Garden Carpet moth Xanthorhoe fluctuata.

ILEX AQUIFOLIUM, HOLLY

Sustains 6 Lepidoptera: Swallow-tailed moth Ourapteryx sambucaria, Privet Hawkmoth Sphinx ligustri, Dun-Bar Cosmia trapezina, Double-striped Pug Gymnoscelis pumilata (flowers), Yellow-barred Brindle Acasis viretata (flowers first, then green berries then leaves), and Holly / Azure Blue Celastrina argiolus in spring (flowers, flower buds, green berries and leaves).

IMPATIENS GLANDULIFERA, HIMALAYAN BALSAM / POLICEMANS HELMETS

Sustains Elephant Hawkmoth Deilephila elpenor.

IMPATIENS NOLI ME TANGERE, YELLOW BALSAM

Flowers rich in nectar.

Sole sustainer of Netted Carpet Eustroma reticulata.

INULA CRITHMOIDES, GOLDEN SAMPHIRE

Sustains Ground Lackey Malacosoma castrensis.

INULA DYSENTERICA, GREATER FLEABANE

Sustains Powdered Quaker Orthosia gracilis.

INULA MONTANA, FLEABANE

Sole sustainer of Small Marbled Eublemma parva (flowers).

IRIS FOETIDISSIMA, GLADDON IRIS / STINKING IRIS

Sustains Rosy Minor Procus literosa (in stems).

Suffer: Angle Shades moth Phogophora meticulosa green or olive brown caterpillars feeding on leaves, flowerbuds and blooms. Flagging leaves with eaten out rhizomes indicate Swift moth caterpillars Hepialus lupulinus.

IRIS PSEUDACORUS, YELLOW IRIS / FLAG

Sustains 9 Lepidoptera larva.

Sole sustainer of Crinan / Irish Ear-Moth Hydraecia crinanesis (in roots and lower stems).

Also sustains: Water Ermine Spilosoma urticae / papyratia, Red Swordgrass Xylena vetusta, Crescent Celaena leucostigma /fibrosa (in stems), Rosy Rustic Hydraecia micacea (in roots), Reed Wainscot Nonagria algae / cannae (in stem), Webb's Wainscot Nonagria sparganii (in leaves), and Gold Spot Plusia festucae.

Suffer: Angle Shades moth Phogophora meticulosa green or olive brown caterpillars feeding on leaves, flowerbuds and blooms. Flagging leaves with eaten out rhizomes indicate Swift moth caterpillars Hepialus lupulinus.

IRIS UNGUICALARIS / STYLOSA, ALGERIAN IRIS

Winter flowers rich in nectar good for butterflies venturing out.

Suffer: Angle Shades moth Phogophora meticulosa green or olive brown caterpillars feeding on leaves, flowerbuds and blooms.

Flagging leaves with eaten out rhizomes indicate Swift moth caterpillars Hepialus lupulinus.

JASIONE MONTANA, SHEEP'S-BIT

Sole sustainer of Jasione Pug Eupithecia denotata / jasioneata (in seed heads).

JASMINUM SPECIES

Winter and summer jasmine sustain: Death's-head Hawkmoth Acherontia atropos, and Common Emerald Hemithea aestivaria / strigata / thymiaria (after hibernation).

JUGLANS REGIA, ENGLISH WALNUT

Surprisingly you may find a somewhat familiar maggot in a walnut as rather rarely these sustain same Codling Moth Cydia pomonella as bothers apples.

JUNCUS ARTICULATUS, JOINTED RUSH

Sustains 6 Lepidoptera larva.

Sole sustainer of Small Rufous Coenobia rufa / despecta (in stems).

The flowers attract adult butterflies of Smoky Wainscot Leucania impura, Southern Wainscot Leucania straminea and Common Wainscot Leucania pallens whose offspring may also feed on foliage.

Also sustains: Vapourer Orgyia antiqua, Antler Cerapteryx graminis, and Small Wainscot Tapinstola / Areostola fulva (in roots and stems).

Juncus squarrosus, HEATH RUSH

Sustains: Vapourer Orgyia antiqua, and Antler Cerapteryx graminis.

Juniperus communis, COMMON JUNIPER

<u>Sole sustainer of 2</u>: Juniper Carpet Thera juniperata, and Edinburgh Pug Eupithecia intricate / helveticaria.

<u>One of two sustainers of 2</u>: Chestnut-coloured Carpet Thera cognata / simulata / coniferata other J. sibirica, and Juniper Pug Eupithecia sobrinata / pusillata other J. sibirica.

Also sustains Scalloped Hazel Gonodontis bidentata.

LABURNUM ANAGYROIDES

Sustains / suffers: Sycamore Apatele aceris, and Buff-Tip Phalera bucephala.

LACTUCA SALIGNA, LEAST / WILLOW LETTUCE

Sustains Small Ranunculus Hadena dysodea / chrysozona (flowers and seeds).

LACTUCA SATIVA, LETTUCE

Sustains: Grey Chi moth Antitype chi, Shark Cucullia umbratica, Broad-barred White Hadena serena (flowers and seeds), and Small Ranunculus Hadena dysodea / chrysozona (flowers and seeds).

Suffers: Small / Garden Swift moth Hepialus lupulinus and both roots and leaves attacked by fat, black striped larvae of Great Yellow Underwing moth Noctua / Tryphaena pronuba.

LACTUCA SERRIOLA, PRICKLY LETTUCE

Sustains: Shark Cucullia umbratica, Vine's Rustic Caradrina ambigua, and Broad-barred White Hadena serena (flowers and seeds).

LACTUCA VIROSA, ACRID LETTUCE

Sustains Small Ranunculus Hadena dysodea / chrysozona (flowers and seeds).

Lamiastrum / Lamium galeobdolon, YELLOW ARCHANGEL

Sustains Speckled Yellow Pseudopanthera macularia.

Lamium album, WHITE DEAD NETTLE

Flowers rich nectar producers over long season.

Sustains 14 Lepidoptera larva: Setaceous Hebrew Character Amathes e-nigrum, Flame Axylia putris, Lesser Broad-border Triphaena lanthina, Broad-bordered Yellow Underwing Lampra fimbriata / fimbria, Brown-Spot Pinion Anchocelis litura, Uncertain Caradrina alsines, Burnished Brass Plusia chrysitis, Gold Spangle Plusia bractea, Plain Golden Y Plusia iota, Beautiful Golden Y Plusia pulchrina, Large Twin-spot Carpet Xanthorhoe quadrifasiata, Green Carpet Colostygia pectinataria / viridaria, Black-veined Moth Siona lineata / dealbata, and Scarlet Tiger Callimorpha dominula.

Lamium purpureum, RED DEAD NETTLE

Sustains 9 Lepidoptera larva: Muslin Cycnia mendica, Lesser Broad-border Triphaena lanthina, Broad-bordered Yellow Underwing Lampra fimbriata / fimbria, Brown-Spot Pinion Anchocelis litura, Uncertain Caradrina alsines, Plain Golden Y Plusia iota, Green Carpet Colostygia pectinataria / viridaria, Speckled Yellow Pseudopanthera macularia, and Scarlet Tiger Callimorpha dominula.

Larix europaea / decidua, LARCH

Sustains 10 Lepidoptera larva.

Sole sustainer of Larch Pug Eupithecia lariciata.

One of two sustainers Ochreous Pug Eupithecia indigata (on the inflorescence and then needle basal scales but not the needles) other being similar on Pinus.

One of two sustainers of 3: Tawny-barred Angle Semiothisa literata other being Pinus, Barred Red Ellopia fasciaria / prosapiaria other being Pinus, and Small Engrailed Ectropis crepuscularia / biundularia other being Betula.

Also sustains: Autumnal Moth Oporinia autumnata, Scalloped Hazel Gonodontis bidentata, Satin Beauty moth Deileptenia ribeata / abietaria, and Bordered White Bupalus piniaria, and Common Footman Eilema lurideola / complanula algae (on lichens on bark and dead wood).

LATHYRUS LATIFOLIUS, WILD PEA / EVERLASTING PEA

Sustains Long Tailed Blue Lampides boeticus (flowers and seeds).

LATHYRUS MONTANUS, TUBEROUS PEA / BITTER-VETCH

Sustains: Wood White Leptidea sinapis, and Scarce Black-neck Lygephila craccae.

LATHYRUS PALUSTRIS, MARSH PEA

One of three sustainers Black-neck Lygephila pastinum others being Astragalus glycphyllos and Vicia cracca.

LATHYRUS PRATENSIS MEADOW VETCHLING

Sustains Wood White Leptidea sinapis.

LECIDEA CONFLUENS, CONFLUENT LICHEN

Sole sustainer of Marbled Beauty Cryphia perla.

LEONTODON AUTUMNALIS, AUTUMN HAWKBIT

One of three sustainers Stout Dart Spaelotis ravida / obscura others being Taraxacum and Rumex species.

Also sustains Shaded Pug Eupithecia subumbrata / scabiosata (flowers).

LEPTURUS INCURVATUS, SEA HARD-GRASS

One of 2 sustainers Sandhill Rustic Luperina nickerlii / gueneei / incerta other being Agropyron.

LICHENS

Fungi combined with algae, see also ALGAE

Sole sustainers of Dew Moth Setina irrorella are those lichens found on seaside stones.

Sole sustainer of Marbled Beauty Cryphia / Bryophila perla is lichen Lecidea confluens, CONFLUENT LICHEN found on walls.

Also sustains Common Footman Eilema lurideola / complanula, especially lichens on walls and gravestones.

Sole sustainer of 2: Marbled Green Cryphia muralis / glandifera are yellow lichens found on trees, which also sustain Scalloped Hazel Gonodontis bidentata.

Parmelia caperata, GOAT'S-HORN LICHEN and Peltigera canina, DOG LICHEN, found mostly on trees sustain the Large / Four-spotted Footman Lithosia quadra, Dingy Footman Eilema griseola, and Northern Footman Eilema sericea / molybdeola.

Lichens found amongst moss thought to sustain Pigmy Footman Eilema pygmaeola / lutarella / pallifrons.

LIGUSTRUM OVALIFOLIUM, PRIVET
Sustains 12 Lepidoptera larvae.

Sole sustainer of Barred Tooth-striped Nothopteryx polycommata

One of two sustainers Small Blood-vein Scopula imitaria other being Lonicera.

One of three sustainers of 2: Waved Umber Hemerophila abruptaria others being Ribes spp. and Syringa, and Engrailed Ectropis bistortata / biundularia / laricaria / crepuscularia others being Betula and Carpinus.

Also sustains: Death's-head Hawkmoth Acherontia atropos, Privet Hawkmoth Sphinx ligustri, Grey Arches Polia nebulosa (after hibernation), Pale Pinion Lithophane socia / petrificata, Coronet Craniophora ligustri, Flame Brocade Trigonophora flammea / empyrea (in last instar), Lilac Beauty Apeira syringaria, and Yellow-barred Brindle Acasis viretata (flowers first, then green berries then leaves).

LILIUM AURATUM
Sustains / suffers Yellow / Gold Tail Euproctis similes / auriflua.

LIMONIUM VULGARE, SEA LAVENDER / STATICE

Sustains: Ground Lackey Malacosoma castrensis, Rosy Rustic Hydraecia micacea, and Rosy Wave moth Scopula emutaria.

LINARIA VULGARIS, YELLOW TOADFLAX

Flowers rich in nectar and pollen.

One of two sustainers Toadflax Pug Eupithecia linariata (in flowers) other being Antirrhinum.

Also sustains: Striped Hawkmoth Celerio livornica, and Marbled Clover Heliothis dipsacea / viriplaca (flowers and seeds).

LISTERA OVATA, TWAYBLADE

Sustains Red Chestnut Cerastis rubricosa.

LITHOSPERMUM ARVENSE, CORN GROMWELL

Sustains Deep Brown Dart Aporophyla lutulenta.

LOLIUM PERENNE, PERENNIAL RYEGRASS, HUNGARIAN GRAZING RYE

Sustains: Wall butterfly Pararge megera, Hedge Brown / Gatekeeper Maniola tithonus, and Meadow Brown Maniola jurtina / janina.

Lolium temulentum, DARNEL

Sustains Dusky Sallow Eremobia ochroleuca (seeds).

Lonicera garden species and hybrids, HONEYSUCKLES

Sustain 10 Lepidoptera larva: Convolvulus Hawkmoth / Herse Sphinx convolvuli, Privet Hawkmoth S. ligustri, Pine Hawkmoth S. / Hyloicus pinastri, Elephant Hawkmoth Deilephila elpenor, Small Elephant Hawkmoth Deilephila porcellus, Lime Hawkmoth Mimas / Smerinthus tiliae, Lychnis / Hadena bicuris, Shark Cucullia umbratica, Dianthaecia capsincola, Silver Y Plusia gamma, and Pale Tussock Dasychira / Dasyclura pudibunda.

Lonicera periclymenum, WOODBINE

Sustains additional 24 Lepidoptera larva.

Sole sustainer of 2: White Admiral Limenitis Camilla / sibylla and Early Grey Xylocampa areola / lithorhiza.

One of two sustainers of 3: Broad-bordered Bee-Hawkmoth Hemaris fuciformis / bombyliformis other being Symphoricarpus, Streamer Anticlea derivata / nigrofasciaria other being Rosa, and Small Blood-vein Scopula imitaria other being Ligustrum.

Also sustains: Marsh / Greasy Fritillary Euphydryas aurinia / artemis, Ingrailed Clay Diarsia festiva / primulae (in spring), Gothic Phalaena typical (after hibernation), Pale-shouldered Brocade Hadena thalassina, Dark Chestnut Conistra ligula / spadicea, Copper Underwing Amphipyra pyramidea, Gold Spangle Plusia bractea, Plain Golden Y Plusia iota, Beautiful Golden Y Plusia pulchrina, Common Emerald Hemithea aestivaria / strigata / thymiaria (after hibernation), Rosy Wave moth Scopula emutaria, Early Tooth-striped Nothopteryx carpinata / lobulata, Early Thorn Selenia bilunaria / illunaria, Lilac Beauty Apeira syringaria, Swallow-tailed moth Ourapteryx sambucaria, Pale Oak Beauty Boarmia punctinalis / consortaria. Suffers Jersey Tiger Euplagia quadripunctaria / hera, and Beautiful Arches Eumichtus satura. Honeysuckle blooms also suffer a micro-Lepidoptera Many-plume moth Orneodes hexadactyla causing the flowers to gall.

LOTUS CORNICULATUS, BIRDSFOOT TREFOIL

Sustains 19 Lepidoptera larva: Common Blue Polyommatus icarus / alexis, Chalkhill Blue Lysandra coridon, Clouded Yellow Colias croceus / edusa, Pale Clouded Yellow Colias hyale, Wood White Leptidea sinapis, Dingy Skipper Erynnis tages, Grass Eggar Lasiocampa trifolii, Burnet Companion Eetypa glyphica, Shaded Broad-Bar Ortholitha chenopodiata / limitata / mensuraria, Hoary Footman Eilema caniola, Chalk Carpet Ortholitha bipunctaria, Ringed Carpet Cleora cinctaria, Straw Belle Aspitates gilvaria, Yellow Belle Aspitates chrearia / citraria, Scarce Black Arches Celama aerugula / centonalis (flowers and leaves), Silver Cloud Xylomiges conspicullaris (flowers), Green Hairstreak Callophrys rubi (flowers and leaves), and Bloxworth Blue Everes argiades / tiresias (flowers, seeds and leaves).

LUNARIA ANNUA / BIENNIS, HONESTY

Flowers rich in nectar.

Sustains / suffers Large White Pieris brassicae.

Lupinus, LUPINS

Suffer: Swift moth Hepialus lupulinus root eating white caterpillars causing slow death, and Dot Melanchra persicariae.

Luzula campestris, FIELD WOOD-RUSH

<u>One of three sustainers</u> Dotted Fanfoot Zanclognatha cribrumalis / cribralis (in stems and leaves) others being Carex sylvatica and Luzula pilosa.

Also sustains: Broad-bordered Yellow Underwing Lampra fimbriata / fimbria, Smoky Wainscot Leucania impura, Double Line Mythimna turca, and may sustain Twin-spot Carpet Colostygia didymata.

Luzula pilosa, HAIRY WOOD-RUSH

Sustains 6 Lepidoptera larva.

<u>One of three sustainers</u> Dotted Fanfoot Zanclognatha cribrumalis / cribralis (in stems and leaves) others being Carex sylvatica and Luzula campetris.

Also sustains: Smoky Wainscot Leucania impure, Double Line Mythimna turca, Common Rustic Apamea secalis / oculea / didyma (in stems), Slender Brindle Apamea scolopacina, and may sustain Twin-spot Carpet Colostygia didymata.

Luzula sylvatica, GREAT WOOD-RUSH

Found in drier habitats than other rushes.

Sustains: Purple Clay Diarsia brunnea, and may sustain Twin-spot Carpet Colostygia didymata.

Lychnis alba, WHITE CAMPION

Evening scented flowers attract Lychnis Hadena bicuris, Coronet Hadena conspersa and other night flying Lepidoptera, which then lay their eggs, the larvae eat the seeds, but not all so both benefit.

Sustains 7 Lepidoptera larva.

Sole sustainers of Rivulet Perizoma affinitata (in seed capsules) are several similar scarce Lychnis species.

One of three sustainers Sandy Carpet Perizoma flavofasciata / decolorata (flowers and seeds) others being other Lychnis species and Silene inflata.

Also sustains: as mentioned above -Marbled Coronet Hadena conspersa / nana, & Lychnis Hadena bicruris / capsincola (unripe seeds), plus Tawny Shears Hadena lepida / carpophaga (unripe seeds), Campion Hadena cucubali (leaves and unripe seeds), and Marbled Clover Heliothis dipsacea /viriplaca (flowers and seeds).

Lychnis dioica, RED CAMPION

Blooms open in daytime closing for night, shorter tube to nectary than white campion provides access to other insects as well as Lepidoptera.

Sustains 8 Lepidoptera larva.

Sole sustainers of Rivulet Perizoma affinitata (in seed capsules) are several similar scarce Lychnis species.

<u>One of three sustainers</u> Sandy Carpet Perizoma flavofasciata / decolorata (flowers and seeds) others being other Lychnis species and Silene inflata.

Also sustains: Marbled Coronet Hadena conspersa / nana, Lychnis Hadena bicruris / capsincola (unripe seeds), Tawny Shears Hadena lepida / carpophaga (unripe seeds), Campion Hadena cucubali (leaves and unripe seeds), Twin-spot Carpet Colostygia didymata, and Netted Pug Eupithecia venosata / insigniata (in seed capsules).

LYCHNIS FLOS-CUCULI, RAGGED ROBIN
<u>Sole sustainers of</u> Rivulet Perizoma affinitata (in seed capsules) are several similar scarce Lychnis species.

Also sustains: Marbled Coronet Hadena conspersa / nana, Lychnis Hadena bicruris / capsincola (unripe seeds), and Campion Hadena cucubali (leaves and unripe seeds).

LYCHNIS GITHAGO (SIC)
Flowers have deep nectary only accessible to Lepidoptera.

LYCIUM BARBARUM, GOJI / DUKE OF ARGYLL'S TEA PLANT
Sustains Death's-head Hawkmoth Acherontia atropos.

LYCOPERSICON ESCULENTUM, TOMATOES
Suffer: Beautiful Brocade Hadena contigua, and Brown Brocade / Bright-line Brown Eye Diataraxia oleracea, Tomato moth Polia oleracea caterpillar, greenish to reddy brown or yellow, up to two inches long, eats the leaves underside first then finishes

whole lot, it eats at night and if disturbed drops, onto waiting sheets of newspaper if you're foresighted.

LYSIMACHIA VULGARIS, YELLOW LOOSESTRIFE

<u>Sole sustainer of</u> Dentated Pug Anticollix sparsata.

Also sustains: Water Ermine Spilosoma urticae / papyratia, Powdered Quaker Orthosia gracilis, Plain Wave Sterrha inornata, and V Pug Chloroclystis coronata (flowers).

LYTHRUM SALICARIA, PURPLE LOOSTRIFE

Flowers are rich in nectar.

Sustains: Small Elephant Hawkmoth Deilephila porcellus, Emperor Saturnia pavonia / carpini, Powdered Quaker Orthosia gracilis, Common Heath-moth Ematurga atomaria, and V Pug Chloroclystis coronata (eats flowers).

Magnolia grandifolia

Sustains Large Ranunculus Antitype flavicincta.

Malus, APPLE

Sustains / suffers 50 Lepidoptera larva.

<u>One of two sustainers of 2</u>: Pinion-spotted Pug Eupithecia insigniata / consignata (eats flowers first) other being Crataegus, and Green Pug Chloroclystis rectangulata (flowers) other being Pyrus.

Also sustains: Scarce Swallow-tail Graphium podalirius, Eyed Hawkmoth Smerinthus ocellata, Lobster Moth Stauropus fagi, Pale Eggar Trichiura crataegii, Small Eggar Eriogaster lanestris, Chinese Character Cilix glaucata / spinula, Triple-spotted Clay Amathes ditrapezium, occasionally Brown Tail Euproctis chrysorrhoea / phaecorrhoea, Lappet Gastropacha quercifolia, Short-Cloaked Nola cucullatella, Least Black Arches Celama confusalis / cristulalis, Gothic Phalaena typical, Sprawler Brachyonycha sphinx / cassinia, Green-Brindled Crescent Allophyes oxycanthae, Dotted Chestnut Dasycampa rubiginea, Dark Dagger Apatele tridens, Lunar-Spotted Pinion Cosmia pyralina, Nut-tree Tussock Colocasia coryli, Figure of Eight Episema caeruleocephala, Blue-bordered Carpet Plemyria bicolorata / rubiginata, Red-green Carpet Chloroclysta siterata / psittacata, and Brimstone Moth Opisthograptis luteolata / crataegata.

Suffers badly from the Codling Moth Cydia pomonella, big holes with 'maggots' in the apples in mid to late summer and a pinkish caterpillar with a brown head, these make a big mess in the middle, often enter from the side of the fruit and leaves by eye, but does at least ruin but the one fruit apiece.

Suffers the Vapourer moth Orgyia antiqua caterpillar, hairy yellow tufts on their backs, leaves egg bundles of 200 yellowish or reddish brown eggs attached with a silk cocoon. Do not touch these caterpillars as the hairs can irritate your skin.

Suffers, and avoid likewise, the Lackey moth Malacosoma neutria, a blueish grey caterpillar with red, and whitish or yellowish stripes, spin themselves a silk tent in midsummer, the eggs are laid in an obvious ring around a stem.

Suffers many Tortrix moths. Caoaecia / Archips podana, fruit-surface eating caterpillars are pale yellow and feed under a leaf they have stuck to the fruit. Cherry Bark Tortrix Enarmonia formosana is a pink caterpillar tunneling under the bark, mainly on cherries but also attacks Malus, Pyrus and Prunus trees especially those in decline. Several other closely related Tortrix moths also eat foliage, buds and damage the surface of fruits. Distinguishable by their wriggling backwards if touched these mostly hide in silk nests formed between leaf surfaces where they hide.

Suffers the Bud moth Spilonata ocellana caterpillars are small reddish brown with a black head and first ruin the buds then the foliage and finally the fruits.

Suffers the Browntail moth Euproctis chrysorrhea, caterpillars are striped red and white and hairy going grey with age, and the Small Ermine Moth Hyponomeuta (probably Yponomeuta evonymella) malinellus / malinella, small spotted caterpillars, both build silk nests in the crutches and branches and venture out to defoliate the tree.

Suffer the Fall Webworm Hyphantria cunea, light green becoming brownish with warts, caterpillars eat the underside of the leaves leaving skeletons while the droppings are caught in masses of hairy webbing they make for protection.

Suffer the Black-veined White butterfly Aporia crataegi yellow caterpillars eat the topside of the leaves and spin them together with loose webs in which they overwinter and when mature pupate attached to twigs.

Suffer the Pith moth Blastodacna atra, larvae are brownish pink with a brown head, these eat out the centres of shoots and buds which die back.

Also suffer three more moth maggots; the Winter moth Operophethora / Operophtera brumata, the March moth Erannis aescularia and the Mottled Umber Hybernia defoliaria. These are all Looper caterpillars and move by making a bend in their middle moving front and rear independently. These damage foliage and fruit from early in the season and then fall to the ground to pupate. The female Winter moth cannot fly and must crawl up the tree to lay eggs.

Suffer Apple Leaf Blister moths Lyonetia clerkella, these are very small, the adults overwinter in bark cracks and lay eggs in young leaves which are mined by green larvae, these fall with leaves in autumn to pupate and overwinter, sometimes bits of leaf drop out, and there can be up to 3 generations a year, also found on Prunus cerasus.

Suffer Apple Fruit miners Argyresthia conjugella, make wee tunnels under the skin causing sunken patches leading to rotten flesh, their alternate host is rowan / mountain ash trees.

Suffer the Leopard moth Zeuzera pyrina caterpillars, yellowish white, brown head and black spots up to two inches long bore in the wood.

Also suffer: Yellow / Gold Tail Euproctis similes / auriflua (also on fruits), Gipsy Moth Lymantria dispar, Black Arches Lymantria monacha, Pale Pinion Lithophane socia / petrificata, and Grey Dagger Apatele psi.

And also suffer the rather different Eupista species and Solenobia inconspicuella, the caterpillars of these make little cigar shaped cases in which they live and feed eating the leaves through the hole in the end making a series of overlapping little round holes making a bigger irregular patch of bare leaf.

Malva sylvestris, COMMON MALLOW

Blooms are rich in nectar.

One of two sustainers Mallow Larentia clavaria / cervinata other being Althea.

One of three sustainers Four-Spotted Acontia luctuosa others being Convolvolus and Plantago.

Also sustains: Painted Lady Vanessa cardui, and Least Yellow Underwing Triphaena interjecta.

Malva rotundifolia, DWARF MALLOW

<u>One of three sustainers</u>: Pale Shoulder Tarache solaris / lucida others being Convolvulus and Glechoma, and Four-Spotted Acontia luctuosa others being Convolvulus and Plantagos.

MAMESTRA brassicae CABBAGE MOTH

see Brassicas. Also attacks marigolds, Dahlias, Geraniums, tobacco, docks and red currants.

Matricaria, WILD CHAMOMILE

This is well confused and conflated in sources with GERMAN CHAMOMILE and with SCENTED MAYWEED, M. recutita and PINEAPPLE MAYWEED, M. matricarioides, and SCENTLESS MAYWEED, Tripleurospermum inodorum / M. inodora

Sustains Lesser Broad-border Triphaena lanthina.

Matricaria chamomilla

Sustains Chamomile Shark Cucullia chamomillae (flowers).

Matthiola species, STOCKS

Sustain Garden Carpet Xanthorhoe fluctuata.

Medicago falcata, SICKLE MEDICK

Sustains: Scarce Black Arches Celama aerugula / centonalis (flowers and leaves), and Grass Eggar Lasiocampa trifolii.

Medicago lupulina, BLACK MEDICK

Sustains 7 Lepidoptera larvae: Common Blue Polyommatus icarus / alexis, Pale Clouded Yellow Colias hyale, Burnet Companion Eetypa glyphica, Chalk Carpet Ortholitha bipunctaria, Latticed Heath Chiasma clathrata, Straw Belle Aspitates gilvaria, and Bloxworth Blue Everes argiades / tiresias (seeds).

Medicago sativa, ALFALFA / LUCERNE

Sustains 7 Lepidoptera larvae: Pale Clouded Yellow Colias hyale, Shears Hada nana / dentina, Clouded Yellow Colias croceus / edusa, Grass Eggar Lasiocampa trifolii, Scarce Bordered Straw Heliothis armigera, Burnet Companion Eetypa glyphica, and Latticed Heath Chiasma clathrata.

Melampyrum arvense, PURPLE COW-WHEAT

One of three sustainers Lead-coloured Pug Eupithecia plumbeolata (flowers) others being Melampyrum pratense and Rhinanthus.

Melampyrum pratense, COMMON COW-WHEAT

One of three sustainers Lead-coloured Pug Eupithecia plumbeolata (flowers) others being Melampyrum arvense and Rhinanthus.

Also sustains Heath Fritillary Melitaea athalia.

Melampyrum sylvaticum, WOOD COW WHEAT

Sustains Heath Fritillary Melitaea athalia.

Melilotus arvensis, FIELD MELILOT

Flowers are rich in nectar.

One of two sustainers Small Blue Cupido minimus / alsus (flowers) other being Anthyllis.

Also sustains: Mazarine Blue Cyaniris semiargus / acis, Clouded Yellow Colias croceus / edusa, Grass Eggar Lasiocampa trifolii, and Mother Shipton Euclidimera mi.

Melilotus officinalis YELLOW MELILOT

Sustains Beaded Chestnut Agrochola lychnidis / pistacina.

Mentha arvensis, CORN MINT

Sustains: Orange Moth Angerona prunaria, and Deep Brown Dart Aporophyla lutulenta.

Mentha aquatica, WATER-MINT

One of two sustainers Pinion-streaked Snout Schranckia costaestrigalis other being Thymus.

Also sustains: Orange Moth Angerona prunaria, and Water Ermine Spilosoma urticae / papyratia.

Menyanthes trifoliata, BUCKBEAN / BOGBEAN

Sustains: Elephant Hawkmoth Deilephila elpenor, and Light Knotgrass Apatele menyanthidis.

Milium effusum, SPREADING MILLET-GRASS

Sustains Ringlet Aphantopus hyperantus.

Molinia caerula, PURPLE MOOR GRASS

Sole sustainer of Marbled White-Spot Jaspidia pygarga / fasciana / fuscula.

One of two sustainers Scotch Argus Erebia aethiops / blandina / medea other being Aira caespitosa.

Also sustains: Large Heath / Marsh Ringlet Coenonympha tullia / davus / tiphon, Drinker Philudoria potatoria, Antler Cerapteryx graminis, and Crescent Celaena leucostigma / fibrosa (in stems).

MOSSES

One of two sustainers Barred Carpet Perizoma taeniata other being Stellaria.

One of three sustainers Dwarf Cream Wave Sterrha fuscovenosa / interjectaria / dilutaria / osseata (in winter) occassionally others usually being Anagallis, Polygonum arvense and Taraxacum.

Myosotis arvensis, FIELD FORGET-ME-NOT

Flowers rich in nectar.

Sustains Crimson-speckled Utetheisa pulchella.

Myrica gale, SWEET GALE / BOG MYRTLE

Sustains 17 Lepidoptera larva.

<u>One of three sustainers of 2:</u> Rosy Marsh Coenophila subrosea others being Salix alba and Salix repens, and Nonconformist Graptolitha lamda others being Salix repens and Vaccinium uliginosum.

Also sustains: Fox Moth Macrothylacia rubi, Clouded Buff Diacrisia sannio / russula, Great Brocade Eurois occulta (after hibernation), Silvery Arches Polia hepatica / tincta (in spring), Beautiful Brocade Hadena contigua, Glaucous Shears Hadena bombycina / glauca, Powdered Quaker Orthosia gracilis, Dark Brocade Eumichtis adusta, Light Knotgrass Apatele menyanthidis, Sweet-Gale Apatele euphorbiae / myricae, Northern Argent and Sable Eulype subhastata, Early Thorn Selenia bilunaria / illunaria, Rannoch Brindled Beauty Poccilopsis lapponaria, Ringed Carpet Cleora cinctaria, and Common Heath-moth Ematurga atomaria.

NARDUS STRICTA, MAT-GRASS

Sole sustainer of Mountain Ringlet Erebia epiphron / cassiope.

One of two sustainers Feathered Gothic Tholera popularis other being Poa.

One of three sustainers of 2: Hedge Rustic Tholera cespitis others being Aira species, and Straw Underwing Thalpolphila matura / eytherea others being Aira and Poa species.

Also sustains: Small Heath Coenonympha pamphilus, and Antler Cerapteryx graminis.

NASTURTIUM OFFICINALE, WATERCRESS

Sustains / suffers: Small White P. rapae, Green-veined White Pieris napi, and Orange-Tip Anthocaris cardamines.

NERIUM OLEANDER

One of three sustainers Oleander Hawkmoth Daphnis nerii others being Cornus mas and Vincas.

NICOTIANA AFFINIS, SWEET TOBACCO

Flowers of most species rich in nectar.

Sustains: Pearly Underwing Peridroma porphyrea / saucia, Scarce Bordered Straw Heliothis armigera, and Mamestra brassicae Cabbage Moth.

Nʏᴍᴘʜᴀᴇᴀ ᴀʟʙᴀ, WHITE WATER-LILY

Sustains Brown China Marks moth (sic, text gives no Latin name) greenish brown caterpillars eating tops of leaves.

— O —

ONOBRYCHIS VICIFOLIA, SAINFOIN / ESPARSETTE

Sustains: Queen of Spain Fritillary Argynnis lathonia, Latticed Heath Chiasma clathrata, and Bloxworth Blue Everes argiades / tiresias (flowers, seeds and leaves).

ONONIS REPENS / ARVENSIS, REST-HARROW

Sustains 14 Lepidoptera larva.

One of two sustainers Rest-Harrow Aplasta ononaria other being Sarothamnus.

One of three sustainers White Colon Heliophobus albicolon (eats flowers) others being Sisymbrium sophia and Convolvulus soldanella.

Also sustains: Silver-Studded Blue Phlebius argus / aegon, Common Blue Polyommatus icarus / alexis, Grass Eggar Lasiocampa trifolii, Small Mottled Willow Laphygma exigua, Bordered Sallow Pyrrhia umbra / marginata (shoots, flowers and seeds), Marbled Clover Heliothis dipsacea /viriplaca (flowers and seeds), Plain Wave Sterrha inornata, Yellow Shell Euphyia bilineata, Yellow Belle Aspitates chrearia / citraria, Portland Moth Actebia praecox, Pale Shining Brown Polia nitens / advena, and Isle of Wight Wave Sterrha humiliata / osseata.

ONONIS REPENS SPINOSA, SPINY REST-HARROW

Sustains 11 Lepidoptera larvae.

One of two sustainers Rest-Harrow Aplasta ononaria other being Sarothamnus.

<u>One of three sustainers</u> White Colon Heliophobus albicolon (eats flowers) others being Sisymbrium sophia and Convolvulus soldanella.

Also sustains: Silver-Studded Blue Phlebius argus / aegon, Common Blue Polyommatus icarus / alexis, Grass Eggar Lasiocampa trifolii, Small Mottled Willow Laphygma exigua, Bordered Sallow Pyrrhia umbra / marginata (shoots, flowers and seeds), Marbled Clover Heliothis dipsacea /viriplaca (flowers and seeds), Plain Wave Sterrha inornata, Yellow Shell Euphyia bilineata, and Yellow Belle Aspitates chrearia / citraria.

ONOPORDUM ACANTHIUM, COTTON THISTLE
Warm up their flower heads to aid pollinators.

Sustains Painted Lady Vanessa cardui, and Myelois cribrella (in stems).

ORIGANUM VULGARE, MARJORAM / OREGANO
Copious flowers rich in nectar.

Sustains 10 Lepidoptera larva.

<u>One of two sustainers</u> Lace Border Scopula ornata / paludata other being Thymus.

Also sustains: White Point Leucania albipuncta, Mullein Wave Scopula marginepunctata / promutata / incanata, Lewes Wave Scopula immorata, Sub-angled Wave Scopula nigropunctata / strigilaria, Green Carpet Colostygia pectinataria / viridaria, Shaded Pug Eupithecia subumbrata / scabiosata, Wormwood Pug Eupithecia absinthiata / minutata, Black-veined Moth Siona lineata / dealbata, and Double-striped Pug Gymnoscelis pumilata (flowers).

ORNITHOPUS PERPUSILLUS, BIRD'S-FOOT

Sustains: Silver-Studded Blue Phlebius argus / aegon, Common Blue Polyommatus icarus / alexis, and Chalkhill Blue Lysandra coridon.

OXALIS ACETOSELLA, WOOD SORREL

Sustains Twin-spot Carpet Colostygia didymata.

PARIETARIA OFFICINALIS, PELLITORY OF THE WALL

<u>One of two sustainers of 2</u>: Bloxworth Snout Hypena obsitalis other being stinging nettle, and Nettle-tap Anthophila fabriciana other being Urtica dioica.

<u>One of three sustainers</u> Red Admiral Vanessa atalanta others being Humulus and Urtica dioica.

PARMELIA CAPERATA, GOAT'S-HORN LICHEN

<u>One of two sustainers of 2</u> Dingy Footman Eilema griseola other being Peltigera, and Northern Footman Eilema sericea / molybdeola other being Peltigera.

Also sustains Large / Four-spotted Footman Lithosia quadra.

PARTHENOCISSUS SPP. VIRGINIA CREEPER

Flowers are rich in nectar.

Sustains Elephant Hawkmoth Deilephila elpenor.

PASSIFLORA SPP. PASSIONFLOWERS

Mostly tender save P. caerula.

Sustains Grey Chi moth Antitype chi.

Pastinaca sativa, PARSNIP

One of three sustainers White-spotted Pug Eupithecia tripunctaria / albipunctata (eats flowers) others being Angelica and Heracleum.

Also sustains Small / Garden Swift Moth Hepialus lupulinus (roots).

Paxillus pannoides, BROWN-RIBBED BRACKET FUNGUS

Sustains Waved Black Parascotia fuliginaria.

Pedicularis palustris, MARSH LOUSEWORT

Parasitic bog plant.

Sustains Water Ermine Spilosoma urticae / papyratia.

Pedicularis sylvatica, LOUSEWORT / RED RATTLE

Semi-parasitic on many plants of heaths and meadows.

One of two sustainers Small Purple-barred Phytometra viridaria / aenea other being Polygala vulgaris.

Pelargonium species NOT GERANIUMS

Sustain Scarce Bordered Straw Heliothis armigera.

Suffers: Angle Shades moth Phogophora meticulosa green or olive brown caterpillars feed on leaves, flowerbuds and blooms, and a new stem caterpillar, Geranium Bronze has arrived here from the Mediterranean region where it has decimated

Pelargoniums, eating it's way down the centre of their stems and shredding leaves and buds.

Peltigera canina, DOG LICHEN
One of two sustainers Dingy Footman Eilema griseola / stramineola other being Parmelia.

Also sustains Large / Four-spotted Footman Lithosia quadra.

Petasites hybridus, BUTTERBUR
Sole sustainer of Butterbur Hydraecia petasitis.

Petroselinum hortense, PARSLEY
Sustains Mouse Amphipyra tragopogonis.

Peucedanum palustre, HOG'S FENNEL
Sustains Swallow-tail Papilio machaon.

Phalaris canariensis, CANARY GRASS
One of two sustainers of 2: Small Clouded Brindle other being Digraphis, and Double Lobed Apamea ophiogramma (in stems) other being Digraphis.

Also sustains Dusky Brocade Apamea obscura / gemina / remissa.

Phleum pratense, TIMOTHY/ CAT'S-TAIL GRASS

One of three sustainers Essex Skipper Thymelicus lineola others being Agropyron repens and Brachypodium pinnatum.

Also sustains: Marbled White Melanargia galathea, Meadow Brown Maniola jurtina / janira, Large Skipper Ochlodes venata / sylvanus, and Small Skipper Thymelicus sylvestris / linea / thaumus.

Phlox species

Suffer Tortrix moth Cephasia species.

Phragmites australis / communis / Arundo phragmites, COMMON REED

Important plants their foliage and parts sustaining 14 Lepidoptera larva.

Sole sustainer of 10: Flame Wainscot Meliana flammea, Fenn's Wainscot Arenostola brevilinea, Fen Wainscot Arenostola phragmitidis (in stem), Twin-Spotted Wainscot Nonagria geminipuncta (in stem), Striped Wainscot Leucania pudorina / impudens, Obscure Wainscot Leucania obsoleta, Large Wainscot Rhizedra lutosa / crassicornis (in stem), Brown-Veined Wainscot Nonagria dissolute / arundineta (in stem), Sussex Wainscot Nonagria neurica / edelsteni (in stem), Silky Wainscot Chilodes maritime / ulvae (on lining of dead reeds and on larvae and pupae of other insects).

One of three sustainers of 2: Reed Dagger / Powdered Wainscot Simyra albovenosa / venosa others being Carex caespitosa and Poa aquatica, and Reed Tussock Laelia caenosa others being

Cladium and Sparganium. Also sustains Smoky Wainscot Leucania impura, and Southern Wainscot Leucania straminea.

PLUS Green algae on dead reeds.

Sole sustainer of Round-winged Muslin Comacla senex.

PHYLLREA SPECIES
Sustains Privet Hawkmoth Sphinx ligustri.

PHYSCIA STELLARIA, STAR LICHEN
One of two sustainers Beautiful Hook-tip Laspeyria flexula other being Xanthoria wall lichen.

PICEA EXCELSA / ABIES, NORWAY SPRUCE
Sustains 8 Lepidoptera larvae.

Sole sustainer of 2: Cloaked Pug Eupithecia pini / togata (on unripe seeds in cones), and Dwarf Pug Eupithecia tantillaria / pusillata / subumbrata.

One of two sustainers of 2: Pine Hawkmoth Hyloicus pinastri other being Lonicera, and Grey Pine Carpet Thera obeliscata other being Pinus.

Also sustains: Satin Beauty moth Deileptenia ribeata / abietaria, Bordered White Bupalus piniaria, and suffers Black Arches Lymantria monacha.

Picris hieracioides, HAWKWEED OX TONGUE

Blooms visited by at least 27, another reference 29, different insect species: 3 butterflies and moths, 16 species bee, 9 species flies and 1 other, also suffers Broad-barred White Hadena serena (flowers and seeds).

PIERIS BRASSICAE, P. napi & P. rapae, CABBAGE WHITE BUTTERFLIES

Large, White and Green Veined most serious pests of brassica family. Do NOT destroy small yellow silky cocoons as these contain the Ichneumon Fly Microgaster glomeratus who will lay about sixty eggs in a Large White caterpillar parasitising it. Another Ichneumon Fly Pteromalus brassicae lays up to two hundred and fifty eggs on the newly formed chrysalis parasitizing it. Wasps also predate these caterpillars, particularly those of Small White.

Pimpinella saxifraga, BURNET-SAXIFRAGE

Blooms attract 23 insect species: 0 butterflies or moths, 3 species bee, 8 species diptera flies and 12 other.

One of two sustainers Pimpinel Pug Eupithecia pimpinellata / denotata (eats flowers) other **P.** major.

One of three sustainers Single-dottted Wave Sterrha dimidiata / scutulata (eats flowers) others being Galium and Anthriscus.

Also sustains: Swallow-tail Papilio machaon, Lime-speck Pug Eupithecia centaureata / oblongata (eats flowers), and Wormwood Pug Eupithecia absinthiata / minutata.

Pimpinella major, GREATER BURNET-SAXIFRAGE

One of two sustainers Pimpinel Pug Eupithecia pimpinellata / denotata (flowers) other P. saxifraga.

Also sustains: Lime-speck Pug Eupithecia centaureata / oblongata (flowers), and Wormwood Pug Eupithecia absinthiata / minutata.

Pinus lauricio-nigricans, AUSTRIAN PINE

One of two sustainers of 8: Pine Beauty Panolis flammea/ piniperda other P. sylvestris, Ochreous Pug Eupithecia indigata (inflorescence and then needle basal scales but not needles) other Larix, Pine Hawkmoth Hyloicus pinastri other Picea, Pine Beauty Panolis flammea / piniperda other P. sylvestris, Grey Pine Carpet Thera obeliscata other Picea, Pine Carpet Thera firmata other Cedrus, Barred Red Ellopia fasciaria / prosapiaria other Larix, and Tawny-barred Angle Semiothisa literata other also being Larix.

One of three sustainers Orange Footman Eilema sororcula / aureola (algae and lichens on bark) others being on Abies and Quercus.

Also sustains: Autumnal Moth Oporinia autumnata, Satin Beauty moth Deileptenia ribeata / abietaria, Bordered White Bupalus piniaria, and suffers Black Arches Lymantria monacha.

Pisum sativum, PEAS

Sustain: Silver Gamma / Y Moth Plusia gamma, Pale Mottled Yellow Caradrina clavipalpis / cubicularis / quadripunctata (seeds), and Scarce Bordered Straw Heliothis armigera.

Suffers Pea Moth Laspeyresia nigricana, those most annoying small greenish white grubs in the peas, very early and very late crops often miss this as the moth is flying in midsummer.

Plantago coronopus, BUCK'S HORN PLANTAIN

Sustains 36 Lepidoptera larvae.

<u>Sole sustainers of</u> Glanville Fritillary Melitaea cinxia are Plantain species.

<u>One of three sustainers of 2</u>: Four-Spotted Acontia luctuosa others being Convolvolus and Plantago, and Rustic Caradrina blanda / taraxaci others being Rumex species and Stellaria chickweed.

Also sustains: Heath Fritillary Melitaea athalia, Muslin Cycnia mendica, Ruby Tiger Phragmatobia fuliginosa, Clouded Buff Diacrisia sannio / russula, Wood Tiger Parasemia plantaginis, Heart and Dart Agrotis exclamationis, Pearly Underwing Peridroma porphyrea / saucia, Barred Chestnut Diarsia dahlii, Flame Shoulder Ochropleura plecta, Setaceous Hebrew Character Amathes e-nigrum, Square-spot Rustic Amathes xanthographa, Flame Axylia putris, Great Brocade Eurois occulta, Lesser Yellow Underwing Triphaena comes / orbona, White-marked Gypsitea leucographa, Silvery Arches Polia hepatica / tincta, White Point Leucania albipuncta, Clay Leucania lithargyria, Deep Brown Dart Aporophyla lutulenta, Uncertain Caradrina alsines, Vine's Rustic Caradrina ambigua, Pale Mottled Yellow Caradrina clavipalpis / cubicularis / quadripunctata, Plain Golden Y Plusia iota, Common Emerald Hemithea aestivaria / strigata / thymiaria (before hibernation), Satin Wave Sterrha subsericeata, Flame Carpet Xanthorhoe designata /

propugnata, Green Carpet Colostygia pectinataria / viridaria, Wormwood Pug Eupithecia absinthiata / minutata, Yellow Belle Aspitates chrearia / citraria, and Lime-speck Pug Eupithecia centaureata / oblongata (seeds), and Red-headed Chestnut Conistra erythrocephala feeds on Quercus species then on Plantagos if underneath.

Suffers Belted Beauty Nyssia zonaria, and Dart Euoxa nigricans.

Plantago lanceolata, RIBWORT PLANTAIN
Sustains 42 Lepidoptera larvae.

<u>Sole sustainers of</u> Glanville Fritillary Melitaea cinxia are Plantain species.

<u>One of three sustainers of 2</u>: Four-Spotted Acontia luctuosa others being Convolvolus and Plantago, and Rustic Caradrina blanda / taraxaci others being Rumex species and Stellaria chickweed.

Also sustains: Heath Fritillary Melitaea athalia, Muslin Cycnia mendica, Ruby Tiger Phragmatobia fuliginosa, Clouded Buff Diacrisia sannio / russula, Wood Tiger Parasemia plantaginis, Heart and Dart Agrotis exclamationis, Pearly Underwing Peridroma porphyrea / saucia, Barred Chestnut Diarsia dahlii, Flame Shoulder Ochropleura plecta, Setaceous Hebrew Character Amathes e-nigrum, Square-spot Rustic Amathes xanthographa, Flame Axylia putris, Great Brocade Eurois occulta, Lesser Yellow Underwing Triphaena comes / orbona, White-marked Gypsitea leucographa, Silvery Arches Polia hepatica / tincta, White Point Leucania albipuncta, Clay Leucania lithargyria, Deep Brown Dart Aporophyla lutulenta, Uncertain Caradrina alsines, Vine's Rustic Caradrina ambigua, Pale Mottled Yellow Caradrina clavipalpis / cubicularis / quadripunctata,

Plain Golden Y Plusia iota, Common Emerald Hemithea aestivaria / strigata / thymiaria (before hibernation), Satin Wave Sterrha subsericeata, Flame Carpet Xanthorhoe designata / propugnata, Green Carpet Colostygia pectinataria / viridaria, Wormwood Pug Eupithecia absinthiata / minutata, Feathered Footman Coscinia striata / grammica, Square-spotted Clay Amathes stigmatica / rhomboides, Six-striped Rustic Amathes sexstrigata / umbrosa, Sweet-Gale Apatele euphorbiae / myricae, Knotgrass moth Apatele rumicis, and Rosy Rustic Hydraecia micacea, and Lime-speck Pug Eupithecia centaureata / oblongata (seeds), and Red-headed Chestnut Conistra erythrocephala feeds on Quercus species then on Plantagos if underneath.

Suffers Belted Beauty Nyssia zonaria, and Dart Euoxa nigricans.

Plus inflorescence sustains Tortrix paleana / icterana forming a loose gall only noticeable by swelling of flower spike, inside up to half a dozen larvae live until they emerge in midsummer leaving their pupal skins stuck between undeveloped flowers.

Plantago major, GREAT PLANTAIN
Sustains 39 Lepidoptera larvae.

Sole sustainer of Treble Lines Maristis trigrammica.

Sole sustainers of Glanville Fritillary Melitaea cinxia are Plantain species.

One of three sustainers of 3: Four-Spotted Acontia luctuosa others being Convolvolus and Plantago, Rustic Caradrina blanda / taraxaci others being Rumex species and Stellaria chickweed, and Dog's Tooth Hadena suasa / dissimillis others being Polygonum arvensis and Rumex species

Also sustains: Heath Fritillary Melitaea athalia, Muslin Cycnia mendica, Ruby Tiger Phragmatobia fuliginosa, Clouded Buff Diacrisia sannio / russula, Wood Tiger Parasemia plantaginis, Heart and Dart Agrotis exclamationis, Pearly Underwing Peridroma porphyrea / saucia, Barred Chestnut Diarsia dahlii, Flame Shoulder Ochropleura plecta, Setaceous Hebrew Character Amathes e-nigrum, Square-spot Rustic Amathes xanthographa, Flame Axylia putris, Great Brocade Eurois occulta, Lesser Yellow Underwing Triphaena comes / orbona, White-marked Gypsitea leucographa, Silvery Arches Polia hepatica / tincta, White Point Leucania albipuncta, Clay Leucania lithargyria, Deep Brown Dart Aporophyla lutulenta, Uncertain Caradrina alsines, Vine's Rustic Caradrina ambigua, Pale Mottled Yellow Caradrina clavipalpis / cubicularis / quadripunctata, Plain Golden Y Plusia iota, Common Emerald Hemithea aestivaria / strigata / thymiaria (before hibernation), Satin Wave Sterrha subsericeata, Flame Carpet Xanthorhoe designata / propugnata, Green Carpet Colostygia pectinataria / viridaria, Wormwood Pug Eupithecia absinthiata / minutata, Silver Cloud Xylomiges conspicullaris, Knotgrass moth Apatele rumicis, and Silver-ground Carpet Xanthorhoe montanata, Lime-speck Pug Eupithecia centaureata / oblongata (seeds), and Red-headed Chestnut Conistra erythrocephala feeds on Quercus species then on Plantagos if underneath.

Suffers Belted Beauty Nyssia zonaria, and Dart Euoxa nigricans.

Plantago maritime, SEA PLANTAIN
Sustains 39 Lepidoptera larvae.

Sole sustainers of Glanville Fritillary Melitaea cinxia are Plantain species.

: Four-Spotted Acontia luctuosa others being Convolvolus and Plantago, and Rustic Caradrina blanda / taraxaci others being Rumex species and Stellaria chickweed.

Also sustains: Heath Fritillary Melitaea athalia, Muslin Cycnia mendica, Ruby Tiger Phragmatobia fuliginosa, Clouded Buff Diacrisia sannio / russula, Wood Tiger Parasemia plantaginis, Heart and Dart Agrotis exclamationis, Pearly Underwing Peridroma porphyrea / saucia, Barred Chestnut Diarsia dahlii, Flame Shoulder Ochropleura plecta, Setaceous Hebrew Character Amathes e-nigrum, Square-spot Rustic Amathes xanthographa, Flame Axylia putris, Great Brocade Eurois occulta, Lesser Yellow Underwing Triphaena comes / orbona, White-marked Gypsitea leucographa, Silvery Arches Polia hepatica / tincta, White Point Leucania albipuncta, Clay Leucania lithargyria, Deep Brown Dart Aporophyla lutulenta, Uncertain Caradrina alsines, Vine's Rustic Caradrina ambigua, Pale Mottled Yellow Caradrina clavipalpis / cubicularis / quadripunctata, Plain Golden Y Plusia iota, Common Emerald Hemithea aestivaria / strigata / thymiaria (before hibernation), Satin Wave Sterrha subsericeata, Flame Carpet Xanthorhoe designata / propugnata, Green Carpet Colostygia pectinataria / viridaria, Wormwood Pug Eupithecia absinthiata / minutata, and Lime-speck Pug Eupithecia centaureata / oblongata (seeds), Ground Lackey Malacosoma castrensis, Feathered Ranunculus Eumichtis lichenea, Sweet-Gale Apatele euphorbiae / myricae, Rosy Rustic Hydraecia micacea, Black-Banded Antitype xanthomista / nigrocincta (flowers and seeds), and Red-headed Chestnut Conistra erythrocephala feeds on Quercus species then on Plantagos if underneath.

Suffers Belted Beauty Nyssia zonaria, and Dart Euoxa nigricans.

Pleurococcus naegelii

Sustains Buff Footman Eilema deplana / helvola / helveola (green algae on Quercus and Betula).

Poa annua, ANNUAL MEADOW GRASS

Sustains 31 Lepidoptera larva.

Sole sustainer of 2: Devonshire Wainscot Leucania putrescens, and Light Arches Apamea lithoxylaea.

One of two sustainers of 5: Feathered Gothic Tholera popularis other being Nardus, Lunar Underwing Omphaloscelis lunosa other being Holcus, Beautiful Gothic Leucochlaena hispida / oditis other being Agropyron, Anomalous Stilbia anomala other being Aira caespitosa, and Ear-Moth Hydraecia oculea / nictitans other Poa species.

One of three sustainers of 2: Dark Arches Apamea monoglypha / polyodon others being Agropyron repens and Dactylis glomerata, and Straw Underwing Thalpolphila matura / eytherea others being Aira and Nardus.

Also sustains: Wall butterfly Pararge megera, Marbled White Melanargia galathea, Hedge Brown / Gatekeeper Maniola tithonus, Ringlet Aphantopus hyperantus (possibly also on other Poa species), Drinker Philudoria potatoria, Antler Cerapteryx graminis, Square-spot Rustic Amathes xanthographa, Deep Brown Dart Aporophyla lutulenta, Grayling Satyrus semele, Common Wainscot Leucania pallens, Feathered Brindle Aporophyla australis, Speckled Wood / Wood Argus Pararge negeria, Southern Wainscot Leucania straminea, Meadow Brown

Maniola jurtina / janira, Small Heath Coenonympha pamphilus, Feathered Ear Pachetra sagittigera / leucophaea, Clay Leucania lithargyria, Double Line Mythimna turca, Dusky Brocade Apamea obscura / gemina / remissa, Silver-Barred Eustrotia olivana / argentula / bankiana, Yellow Shell Euphyia bilineata, and possibly Reddish Light Arches Apamea sublustris though this may also eat other grasses.

POA ALPINA, ALPINE MEADOW-GRASS

Sole sustainer of Northern Arches Apamea exulis / assimilis.

POA AQUATICA, REED MEADOW-GRASS

One of 3 sustainers Reed Dagger / Powdered Wainscot Simyra albovenosa / venosa others being Carex caespitosa and Phragmites australis.

Also sustains: Small Wainscot Arenostola pygmina / fulva (in flower stem), and Silver-Barred Eustrotia olivana / argentula / bankiana.

POA DISTANS, REFLEXED MEADOW-GRASS

One of two sustainers Crescent-Striped Apamea oblonga / abjecta / nigricans other Poa species.

POA MARITIMA, SEA MEADOW-GRASS

Sole sustainer of Mathew's Wainscot Leucania favicolor (may eat other grasses).

One of two sustainers of 2: Crescent-Striped Apamea oblonga / abjecta / nigricans other Poa species, and Ear-Moth Hydraecia oculea / nictitans other Poa species.

Poa nemoralis, WOOD MEADOW GRASS

Sustains 7 Lepidoptera larvae: Speckled Wood / Wood Argus Pararge negeria, Southern Wainscot Leucania straminea, Small Heath Coenonympha pamphilus, Feathered Ear Pachetra sagittigera / leucophaea, Clay Leucania lithargyria, Double Line Mythimna turca, and Confused Apammea furva.

Poa pratensis, BLUEGRASS / SMOOTH-STALKED MEADOW-GRASS

Sustains: Meadow Brown Maniola jurtina / janina, Silver-Barred Eustrotia olivana / argentula / bankiana, and Shaded Broad-Bar Ortholitha chenopodiata / limitata / mensuraria.

Poa trivialis, ROUGHISH / ROUGH-STALKED MEADOW GRASS

Sustains: Speckled Wood / Wood Argus Pararge negeria, Southern Wainscot Leucania straminea, Grayling Satyrus semele, Meadow Brown Maniola jurtina / janina, and Confused Apammea furva.

Polygala vulgaris, MILKWORT

One of two sustainers Small Purple-barred Phytometra viridaria / aenea the other being Pedicularis sylvatica.

Polygonum arvensis, KNOTGRASS

Sustains 40 Lepidoptera larva.

One of two sustainers of 3: Small Fan-footed Wave Sterrha biselata / bisetata (withered leaves) other being Taraxacum officinale, Vestal Rhodometra sacraria other being Anthemis,

Bird's-Wing Dipterygia scabriuscula / pinastri other being Rumex species.

One of three sustainers of 3: Shuttle-Shaped Dart Agrotis puta / radius others being Rumex species and Taraxacum, Dog's Tooth Hadena suasa / dissimillis others being Rumex species and Plantago major, and Dwarf Cream Wave Sterrha fuscovenosa / interjectaria / dilutaria / osseata others being Anagallis and Taraxacum and possibly mosses overwinter.

Also sustains: Dark Swordgrass Agrotis ipsilon / suffusa, Dotted Rustic Rhyacia simulans / pyrophila, Ingrailed Clay Diarsia festiva / primulae, Flame Shoulder Ochropleura plecta, Flame Axylia putris, Green Arches Anaplectoides prasina / herbida, Silvery Arches Polia hepatica / tincta, Pale Shining Brown Polia nitens / advena, Shears Hada nana / dentina, Nutmeg Hadena Trifolii / chenopodii, Beautiful Brocade Hadena contigua, Glaucous Shears Hadena bombycina / glauca, Silver Cloud Xylomiges conspicullaris, Dark Brocade Eumichtis adusta, Knotgrass moth Apatele rumicis, Striped Hawkmoth Celerio livornica, Heart And Club Agrotis clavis / corticea, Light Brocade Hadena w-latinum / genistae, Orache Trachea atriplicis, Mottled Rustic Caradrina morpheus, Common Emerald Hemithea aestivaria / strigata / thymiaria (before hibernation), Isle of Wight Wave Sterrha humiliata / osseata, Satin Wave Sterrha subsericeata, Small Scallop Sterrha emarginata, Riband Wave Sterrha aversata, Lewes Wave Scopula immorata, Blood-vein Calothysanis amata / amataria, Red Twin-spot Carpet Xanthorhoe spadicearia / ferrugata, Gem moth Nycterosea obstipata / fluviata / gemmata, Straw Belle Aspitates gilvaria, Belted Beauty Nyssia zonaria, Satyr Pug Eupithecia satyrata (flowers), and possible sustainer Dotted-Border Wave Sterrha sylvestraria / straminata, and Portland Ribbon Wave Sterrha degeneraria.

POLYGONUM PERSICARIA, REDSHANK / PERSICARIA / SPOTTED PERSICARY

Sustains 6 Lepidoptera larva: Striped Hawkmoth Celerio livornica, Heart And Club Agrotis clavis / corticea, Light Brocade Hadena w-latinum / genistae, Orache Trachea atriplicis, Blood-vein Calothysanis amata / amataria, and Gem moth Nycterosea obstipata / fluviata / gemmate.

POLYPORUS

P. betulinus, and P. schweinitzii, BIRCH BRACKET FUNGUS, and BROWN BRACKET FUNGUS, both sustain Waved Black Parascotia fuliginaria.

POLYSTICTUS

P. abietinus & P. versicolour, PINE BRACKET FUNGUS, and MANY-COLOURED BRACKET FUNGUS, both sustain Waved Black Parascotia fuliginaria.

POPULUS ALBA, ABELE / WHITE POPLAR

Sustains 15 Lepidoptera larva.

Sole sustainers of Figure of Eighty Tethea ocularis / octogesima are Populus species.

One of two sustainers Clifden Nonpareil Catocala fraxini the other being P. nigra.

Also sustains: Swallow Prominent Pheosia tremula / dictaea, Chocolate-Tip Clostera curtula, Seraphim Lobophora halterata / hexapterata, Eyed Hawkmoth Smerinthus ocellatus / ocellata, Pebble Prominent Nodonta ziczac, Sprawler Brachyonycha sphinx / cassinia, Swordgrass Xylena exsoleta, Poplar Grey Apatele megacephala, May Highflyer Hydriomena coerulata / impluviata / trifasciata, Double-striped Pug Gymnoscelis pumilata (eats flowers), and Goat Moth Cossus ligniperda (wood live and dead).

Suffers moth Gypsonoma aceriana / Hedya / Spilonota which makes one gall per stem, about an inch or just under long, the caterpillar eats at the pith and pushes its droppings out a hole, some stick on the stem, after the causer has left the stem may continue in growth in the same direction without branching but the gall often cracks the stem longitudinally and the cavity may enlarge and be used by other critters or become infected by disease.

POPULUS BALSAMIFERA, CANADIAN POPLAR
Sustains 10 Lepidoptera larva.

Sole sustainers of Figure of Eighty Tethea ocularis / octogesima are Populus species

Sustains: Pussmoth Cerura vinula, Miller Apatele leporina, Eyed Hawkmoth Smerinthus ocellatus / ocellata, Pebble Prominent Nodonta ziczac, Sprawler Brachyonycha sphinx / cassinia, Swordgrass Xylena exsoleta, Poplar Grey Apatele megacephala, May Highflyer Hydriomena coerulata / impluviata / trifasciata, and Goat Moth Cossus ligniperda (wood live and dead).

POPULUS FASTIGIATA, LOMBARDY POPLAR
Sustains 13 Lepidoptera larva.

<u>Sole sustainers of</u> Figure of Eighty Tethea ocularis / octogesima are Populus species

Sustains: Pussmoth Cerura vinula, Camberwell Beauty Nymphalis antiopa, Poplar Hawkmoth Laothoe / Smerinthus populi, Poplar Kitten Harpyia hermelina / bifida, Pale Prominent Pterostoma palpina, Eyed Hawkmoth Smerinthus ocellatus / ocellata, Pebble Prominent Nodonta ziczac, Sprawler Brachyonycha sphinx / cassinia, Swordgrass Xylena exsoleta, Poplar Grey Apatele megacephala, May Highflyer Hydriomena coerulata / impluviata / trifasciata, and Goat Moth Cossus ligniperda (wood live and dead).

POPULUS NIGRA, BLACK POPLAR

Sustains 43 Lepidoptera larva.

<u>Sole sustainer of 2:</u> Pale-Lemon Sallow Cirrhia ocellaris (catkins first), and Figure of Eighty Tethea ocularis / octogesima only on Populus species

<u>One of two sustainers of 8</u>: Scarce Chocolate-tip Clostera anachoreta other being Salix caprea, Three Humped Prominent Notodonta tritophus / trilophus / phoebe other P. tremula, Large Dark Prominent Notodonta torva other P. tremula, Poplar Lutestring Tethea or other P. tremula, Lead-coloured Drab Orthosia populeti other P. tremula, Olive Zenobia subtusa other P. tremula, Clifden Nonpareil Catocala fraxini other P. tremula, and Dingy Shears Apamea ypsillon / fissipuncta other being Salix species.

<u>One of three sustainers of 2</u>: Sallow Moth Cirrhia icteritia /fulvago /cerago(catkins first) others being Salix caprea and Salix atrocinerea, and Suspected Parastichtis suspecta others being Betula and Salix species.

Also sustains: Poplar Kitten Harpyia hermelina / bifida, Miller Apatele leporina, Pussmoth Cerura vinula, Camberwell Beauty Nymphalis antiopa, Poplar Hawkmoth Laothoe / Smerinthus populi, Pale Prominent Pterostoma palpina, Swallow Prominent Pheosia tremula / dictaea, Chocolate-Tip Clostera curtula, Dusky Marbled Brown Gluphisia crenata, White Satin Leucoma salicis, December Moth Poecilo campapopuli, Common Quaker Orthosia stabilis, Clouded Drab Orthosia incerta / instabilis, Powdered Quaker Orthosia gracilis, Yellow-Line Quaker Agrochola macilenta, Copper Underwing Amphipyra pyramidea, Minor Shoulder-knot Bombycia viminalis, Double Kidney Zenobia retusa, Red Underwing Catocala nupta, Herald Scoliopteryx libatrix, Clouded Border Lomaspilis marginata, Bordered Beauty Epione repandaria / apiciaria, Eyed Hawkmoth Smerinthus ocellatus / ocellata, Pebble Prominent Nodonta ziczac, Sprawler Brachyonycha sphinx / cassinia, Swordgrass Xylena exsoleta, Poplar Grey Apatele megacephala, May Highflyer Hydriomena coerulata / impluviata / trifasciata, and Goat Moth Cossus ligniperda (wood live and dead). Occasionally sustains: Large Tortoiseshell Nymphalis polychloros, and Brick Agrochola circellaris / ferruginea (buds and catkins)

Suffers Black Arches Lymantria monacha.

POPULUS TREMULA, ASPEN
Sustains 37 Lepidoptera larva.

Sole sustainer of 2 Light Orange Underwing Archiearis notha, and Figure of Eighty Tethea ocularis / octogesima only on Populus species.

One of two sustainers of 7: Three Humped Prominent Notodonta tritophus / trilophus / phoebe other being P. nigra, Large Dark Prominent Notodonta torva other P. nigra, Poplar Lutestring

Tethea or other P. nigra, Lead-coloured Drab Orthosia populeti other P. nigra, Angle-Striped Sallow Enargia paleacea / fulvago other being Betula, Olive Zenobia subtusa other P. nigra, Clifden Nonpareil Catocala fraxini other P. nigra.

Also sustains: Miller Apatele leporina, Pussmoth Cerura vinula, Camberwell Beauty Nymphalis antiopa, Poplar Hawkmoth Laothoe / Smerinthus populi, Poplar Kitten Harpyia hermelina / bifida, Pale Prominent Pterostoma palpina, Swallow Prominent Pheosia tremula / dictaea, Chocolate-Tip Clostera curtula, Coxcomb Prominent Lophopteryx capucina / camelina, Small Chocolate-tip Clostera pigra / reclusa, Twin-Spotted Quaker Orthosia munda, Minor Shoulder-knot Bombycia viminalis, Lesser Belle Colobochyla salicalis, Chevron Lygris testate, Scallop Shell Calocalpe undulata, Seraphim Lobophora halterata / hexapterata, Dark Bordered Beauty Epione vespertaria / parallelaria, Autumnal Moth Oporinia autumnata, Clouded Border Lomaspilis marginata, Eyed Hawkmoth Smerinthus ocellatus / ocellata, Pebble Prominent Nodonta ziczac, Sprawler Brachyonycha sphinx / cassinia, Swordgrass Xylena exsoleta, Poplar Grey Apatele megacephala, May Highflyer Hydriomena coerulata / impluviata / trifasciata, Brick Agrochola circellaris / ferruginea (buds and or catkins), and Goat Moth Cossus ligniperda (wood live and dead).

Occasionally sustains: Large Tortoiseshell Nymphalis polychloros, and Purple Emperor Apatura iris.

Suffers Black Arches Lymantria monacha.

POTENTILLA ANSERINA, SILVERWEED

Sustains: Grizzled Skipper Pyrgus malvae / alveolus, Common Emerald Hemithea aestivaria / strigata / thymiaria, Scarce Black Arches Celama aerugula / centonalis (flowers and leaves), and Rosy Marbled Hapalotis venustula (flowers).

POTENTILLA ERECTA, TORMENTIL

Sustains: Grizzled Skipper Pyrgus malvae / alveolus, Common Emerald Hemithea aestivaria / strigata / thymiaria, Rosy Marbled Hapalotis venustula (flowers), and Small Grass Emerald Chlorissa viridata.

POTENTILLA REPTANS, CREEPING CINQUEFOIL

Sustains 8 Lepidoptera larva: Grizzled Skipper Pyrgus malvae / alveolus, Common Emerald Hemithea aestivaria / strigata / thymiaria, Kent Black-Arches Nola albula / albulalis, Lunar Yellow Underwing Triphaena orbona / subsequa, Rosy Marbled Hapalotis venustula (flowers), Mullein Wave Scopula marginepunctata / promutata / incanata, Annulet Gnophos obscurata / pullata, and Straw Belle Aspitates gilvaria.

POTENTILLA STERILIS, STRAWBERRY-LEAVED CINQUEFOIL

Sustains: Grizzled Skipper Pyrgus malvae / alveolus, Common Emerald Hemithea aestivaria / strigata / thymiaria, Least Yellow Underwing Triphaena interjecta, and Deep Brown Dart Aporophyla lutulenta.

POTERIUM SANGUISORBA, SALAD BURNET

One of two sustainers Reddish Buff Acosmetia caliginosa other being Serratula tinctoria.

Also sustains: Wood Tiger Parasemia plantaginis, Ashworth's Rustic Amathes ashworthii, Feathered Ranunculus Eumichtis lichenea, and Annulet Gnophos obscurata / pullata.

PRIMULA ELATIOR, OXSLIP

<u>Sole sustainer of</u> Duke of Burgundy Hamearis lucina.

Also sustains Plain Clay Amathes depuncts.

Suffers Angle Shades moth.

PRIMULA VERIS, COWSLIP

<u>Sole sustainer of</u> Duke of Burgundy Hamearis lucina.

<u>One of three sustainers</u> Clouded-Bordered Brindle Apamea crenata /rurea others being Primula below and Aira.

Also sustains: Northern Rustic Ammogrotis lucernea, Lunar Yellow Underwing Triphaena orbona / subsequa, and Plain Clay Amathes depuncts.

Also suffers Angle Shades moth.

PRIMULA VULGARIS, PRIMROSE

Sustains 24 Lepidoptera larva.

<u>Sole sustainer of</u> Duke of Burgundy Hamearis lucina.

<u>One of three sustainers</u>: Clouded-Bordered Brindle Apamea crenata / rurea others being Primula above and Aira.

Also sustains: Ingrailed Clay Diarsia festiva / primulae, Dotted Clay Amathes baia, Triple-spotted Clay Amathes ditrapezium, Double Square-spot Amathes triangulum, Square-spotted Clay Amathes stigmatica / rhomboides, Square-spot Rustic Amathes /

Noctua xanthographa / zantographa (eats flowers), Green Arches Anaplectoides prasina / herbida, Great Brocade Eurois occulta, Lesser Broad-border Yellow Underwing Triphaena ianthina, Broad-bordered Yellow Underwing Lampra / Triphaena fimbriata / fimbria, Gothic Phalaena typica (after hibernation), Feathered Ranunculus Eumichtis lichenea, Plain Clay Amathes depuncts, Uncertain Caradrina alsines, Vine's Rustic Caradrina ambigua, Riband Wave Sterrha aversata, Large Twin-spot Carpet Xanthorhoe quadrifasiata, Silver-ground Carpet Xanthorhoe montanata, and Twin-spot Carpet Colostygia didymata.

Also suffers Angle Shades moth.

Prunella vulgaris, SELF-HEAL

Sustains Shaded Pug Eupithecia subumbrata / scabiosata (flowers).

Prunus armeniaca, APRICOT

Sustains Large Ranunculus Antitype flavicincta.

Suffers: usual Winter and Tortrix moths, Small Eggar Eriogaster lanestris, Old Lady Mormo maura, and Figure of Eight Episema caeruleocephala.

Prunus avium, GEAN / MAZZARD / WILD CHERRY / CHERRY

Sustain 26 Lepidoptera larva.

<u>One of two sustainers</u> White Pinion-spotted Bapta bimaculata / taminata other being Crataegus oxycantha.

Also sustains: Large Tortoiseshell Nymphalis polychloros, Black-veined White Aporia crataegi and like most cherries suffers Scarce Swallow-tail Graphium podalirius and Grey Arches Polia nebulosa (after hibernation).

Cherry Fruit moth Argyresthia curvella / nitidella caterpillars, clear green with brown head, enter the flowerbuds and eat those and the fruitlets, fall to ground pupate and emerge within two months to lay eggs in bark crevices and bud scales, the larvae emerge in two batches, some immediately when they eat till they overwinter in silk cocoons hidden in the bark, and another set that wait to hatch later in spring.

Cherry Bark Tortrix Enarmonia formosana is a pink caterpillar tunneling under the bark, may also attack apple, pear and plum trees especially those in decline.

Likewise Apple Leaf Blister moths Lyonetia clerkella are also found on cherries, very small, the adults overwinter in bark cracks and lay eggs in young leaves which are mined by green larvae, these fall with leaves in autumn to pupate and overwinter, sometimes bits of leaf drop out, and there can be up to 3 generations a year.

Occassionally sustains: Alsophila aescularia, Coleophora coracipennella, Cydia funebrana, Epinotia signatana, Hedya dimidioalba, H. pruniana, Lomographa bimaculata, Pandemis cerasana, Scythropia crataegella, Swammerdamia caesiella, and Yponmeuta padella.

Suffers: Small Eggar Eriogaster lanestris, Old Lady Mormo maura, and Figure of Eight Episema caeruleocephala.

Prunus cerasus, SOUR CHERRY

Sustains 24 Lepidoptera larva: Green-Brindled Crescent Allophyes oxyacanthae, Blue-bordered Carpet Plemyria bicolorata / rubiginata, Red-green Carpet Chloroclysta siterata / psittacata, and Barred Umber Anagoga pulveraria.

Occassionally sustains: Acleris notana, Adoxophyes orana, Argyresthia pruniella, Cydia funebrana, C. prunivorana, Epiblema trimaculana, Lyonetia clerkella, Pammene germmana, P. rhediella, Pandemis cerasana, Phyllonorycter sorbi, Stigmella prunetorum, Swammerdamia caesiella, S. pyrella, Tischeria guanacella, and Triphosa dubitata.

Suffers: Small Eggar Eriogaster lanestris, Old Lady Mormo maura, and Figure of Eight Episema caeruleocephala.

Prunus domestica, PLUM / DAMSON / GAGE

Sustains 25 Lepidoptera larva: Scarce Swallow-tail Graphium podalirius, Black-veined White Aporia crataegi, Lappet Gastropacha quercifolia, Large Ranunculus Antitype flavicincta, Short-Cloaked Nola cucullatella, Twin-Spotted Quaker Orthosia munda, Dark Dagger Apatele tridens, Sycamore Apatele aceris, Red Underwing Catocala nupta, Blue-bordered Carpet Plemyria bicolorata / rubiginata, Copper Underwing Amphipyra pyramidea, and occasionally Brown Tail Euproctis chrysorrhoea / phaecorrhoea.

Commonest Lepidoptera co-life is usually the Plum Fruit moth Laspeyresia funebrana whose pinkish larvae are usually found inside very early ripening fruits, the larvae fall to pupate and start a second generation which after ruining more fruit overwinter in cocoons in the ground.

Suffers: most of the caterpillars that bother apples as these also attack plums: Leopard moths, Lackey moths, Winter moths, Tortrix moths, occasionally an errant Codling Moth, Gipsy Moth Lymantria dispar, Cream-spot Tiger Arctia villica, Pale Pinion Lithophane socia / petrificata, Grey Dagger Apatele psi, Small Eggar Eriogaster lanestris, Old Lady Mormo maura, and Figure of Eight Episema caeruleocephala.

PRUNUS INSTITIA, BULLACE

Sustains: Dotted Chestnut Dasycampa rubiginea, Dark Chestnut Conistra ligula / spadicea, and Lunar-Spotted Pinion Cosmia pyralina.

Suffers: Small Eggar Eriogaster lanestris, Old Lady Mormo maura, and Figure of Eight Episema caeruleocephala.

PRUNUS LAUROCERASUS, CHERRY LAUREL

Flowers rich in nectar.

Sustains: Hebrew Character Orthosia gothica, Willow Beauty Alcis rhomboidaria / gemmaria, and occassionally sustains: Acleris rhombana, Diloba caeruleocephala, and Enarmonia formosana.

Suffers: Small Eggar Eriogaster lanestris, Old Lady Mormo maura, and Figure of Eight Episema caeruleocephala.

PRUNUS PADUS, BIRD CHERRY / HAGBERRY

Sustains 15 Lepidoptera larva.

One of three sustainers of 2: Clouded Silver Bapta temerata / punctata others being Betula and Prunus spinosa, and Dotted Clay Amathes baia (in spring), Tissue Triphosa dubitata others being Rhamnus cathartica and R. frangula.

Also sustains: Magpie Abraxas grossulariata, Winter moth Operophtera brumata (and buds), Yponomeuta evonymella which is probably Small Ermine Moth Hyponomeuta malinellus / malinella, and occassionally: Lomographa temerata, Acleris umbrana, Xestia baja, Phtheochroa schreibersiana (and shoots), Epinotia signatana (and shoots), browny black head on yellowish body. Plus, the foliage is mined by micro Lepidoptera Phyllonorycta sorbi.

Suffers: Small Eggar Eriogaster lanestris, Old Lady Mormo maura, and Figure of Eight Episema caeruleocephala.

Prunus persica, PEACH / NECTARINE
Suffer: usual Winter and Tortrix moth culprits and Knotgrass Apatele rumicis, Small Eggar Eriogaster lanestris, Old Lady Mormo maura, and Figure of Eight Episema caeruleocephala.

Prunus spinosa, BLACKTHORN / SLOE
Sustains 66 Lepidoptera larva.

Sole sustainer of 3: Sloe Carpet Bapta distinctata / pictaria, Brown Hairstreak Thecla betulae, and Grey Arches Polia nebulosa.

One of two sustainers Marsh Dagger Apatele strigosa other being Crataegus oxycantha.

One of three sustainers of 4: Common Footman Eilema lurideola / complanula, Scarce Footman Eilema complana (algae and lichens on bark and dead wood) others being algae and lichens on Abies and Rubus species, Clouded Silver Bapta temerata / punctata others being Betula and Prunus padus, Sharp-angled Peacock Semiothisa alternaria / alternata others being Alnus and

Salix caprea, and Early Moth Theria rupicapraria others being Crataegus and Vaccinium myrtillus.

Also sustains: Black Hairstreak Strymonidia pruni, Scarce Swallow-tail Graphium podalirius, Black-veined White Aporia crataegi, Lobster Moth Stauropus fagi, Scarce Vapourer Orgyia recens / gonostigma, Brown Tail Euproctis chrysorrhoea / phaecorrhoea, Pale Eggar Trichiura crataegii, Small Eggar Eriogaster lanestris, Oak Eggar Lasiocampa quercus, Lappet Gastropacha quercifolia, Chinese Character Cilix glaucata / spinula, Short-Cloaked Nola cucullatella, Least Black Arches Celama confusalis / cristulalis, Gothic Phalaena typical, Clouded Drab Orthosia incerta / instabilis, Powdered Quaker Orthosia gracilis, Sprawler Brachyonycha sphinx / cassinia, Green-Brindled Crescent Allophyes oxyacanthae, Satellite Eupsilia transversa / satellitia, Dotted Chestnut Dasycampa rubiginea, Dark Chestnut Conistra ligula / spadicea, Dark Dagger Apatele tridens, Lunar-Spotted Pinion Cosmia pyralina, Nut-tree Tussock Colocasia coryl, Figure of Eight Episema caeruleocephala, Sussex Emerald Thalera fimbrialis, Little Emerald Iodis lactaearia, Broken-barred Carpet Electrophaeus corylata, Blue-bordered Carpet Plemyria bicolorata / rubiginata, Red-green Carpet Chloroclysta siterata / psittacata, Mottled Pug Eupithecia exiguata, November Moth Oporinia dilutata / nebulata, Waved Carpet Hydrelia testaceata / sylvata, Magpie Abraxas grossulariata, Lunar Thorn Selenia lunaria, Brimstone Moth Opisthograptis luteolata / crataegata, Grass Wave Perconia strigillaria, and occasionally Blossom Underwing Orthosia miniosa

Sustains in spring or after hibernation Double Dart Graphiphora augur, Ingrailed Clay Diarsia festiva / primulae, Dotted Clay Amathes baia, Flame Brocade Trigonophora flammea / empyrea (in last instar), Double Square-spot Amathes triangulum, Great Brocade Eurois occulta, Broad-bordered Yellow Underwing Lampra fimbriata / fimbria, Old Lady Mormo maura, Deep Brown Dart Aporophyla lutulenta (unexpanded leaf buds), and Common Emerald Hemithea aestivaria / strigata / thymiaria.

Suffers: Small Eggar Eriogaster lanestris, Old Lady Mormo maura, and Figure of Eight Episema caeruleocephala, Gipsy Moth Lymantria dispar, Emperor Saturnia pavonia / carpini, Scarlet Tiger Panaxia dominula, Hebrew Character Orthosia gothica, Beautiful Arches Eumichtus satura, and Grey Dagger Apatele psi.

Psamma arenaria, MARAM / MARRAN GRASS

<u>One of two sustainers</u> Shore Wainscot Leucania litoralis other being P. baltica.

Also sustains: Grayling Satyrus semele, and Portland Moth Actebia praecox.

Psamma baltica, BALTIC MATWEED

<u>One of two sustainers</u> Shore Wainscot Leucania litoralis other being P. arenaria above.

Pseudotsuga douglasii, DOUGLAS FIR

<u>One of three sustainers</u> Spruce Carpet Thera variata others being Abies species.

Pteris / Pteridium aquilinum, BRACKEN / BRAKE

Sustains 8 Lepidoptera larva.

<u>Sole sustainer of</u> Brown Silver-line Lithina chlorosata / petraria.

Also sustains: Purple Clay Diarsia brunnea, Beautiful Brocade Hadena contigua, Small Angle-Shades Euplexia lucipara, Northern Swift Hepialus velleda (on roots), Gold Swift Hepialus hectus (on roots), and suffers serious attacks by Dot Melanchra persicariae, and Grey Dagger Apatele psi.

PYRUS COMMUNIS, PEARS

Sustain 17 Lepidoptera larva.

<u>One of two sustainers</u> Green Pug Chloroclystis rectangulata (flowers) other being Malus.

Also sustain: Large Tortoiseshell Nymphalis polychloros, Scarce Swallow-tail Graphium podalirius, Lappet Gastropacha quercifolia, Chinese Character Cilix glaucata / spinula, Short-Cloaked Nola cucullatella, Gothic Phalaena typica, Pale-shouldered Brocade Hadena thalassina, Clouded Drab Orthosia incerta / instabilis, Dark Dagger Apatele tridens, occasionally Brown Tail Euproctis chrysorrhoea / phaecorrhoea.

Suffer Summer Fruit Tortrix moths Cacoecia reticulana whose overwintering larvae eat leaves then pupate to emerge and lay eggs in early summer, the hatching larvae web a leaf together, usually to a fruit, and feed inside on leaf and fruit, these mature pupate and lay so that the next generation hatch in early autumn to feed before overwintering.

Cherry Bark Tortrix Enarmonia formosana is a pink caterpillar tunneling under the bark, usually on cherries this also attacks apple, pear and plum trees especially those in decline.

Also suffer: Yellow / Gold Tail Euproctis similes / auriflua, Gipsy Moth Lymantria dispar, and Grey Dagger Apatele psi.

Quercus, OAKS

Sustain 11 Lepidoptera larva on most species.

<u>Sole sustainer</u> Rosy Footman Miltochrista miniata (algae, lichens and dead leaves).

<u>One of two sustainers</u> Speckled Beauty Alcis arenaria / angularia / viduata (algae and lichens) other being lichens on Betula.

<u>One of three sustainers</u> Orange Footman Eilema sororcula / aureola (algae and lichens) others being on Abies and Pinus.

Sustains: Red-necked Footman Atolmis rubricollis (green algae on bark and dead wood), Buff Footman Eilema deplana / helvola / helveola (green algae on bark and dead wood), Large / Four-spotted Footman Lithosia quadra (green algae and lichen on bark and dead wood), Common Footman Eilema lurideola / complanula (green algae and lichen on bark and dead wood),

and probably sustains Olive Crescent Trisateles emortualis (dead leaves and lichens).

Suffers: the Blossom Underwing Orthosia miniosa feeds first on oak leaves then finally on the galls Spathegaster baccarum and Teras terminalis, Red-Headed Chestnut Conistra erythrocephala feeds on oak first then on herbaceous plants underneath, and the Green Oak tortrix moth, Tortrix viridana, may sometimes reach plague proportions and completely defoliate the trees, oaks thus put on what is termed Lammas growth, a new set of leaves in late summer.

Quercus ilex, HOLM / EVERGREEN OAK

One of two sustainers Alchemist Catephia alchymista (in late spring) other being Ulmus.

Occasionally sustains Privet Hawkmoth Sphinx ligustri.

Quercus petraea, SESSILE OAK, and Q. robur, PEDUNCULATE OAK

Similar with very similar co-lives.

Sustain 92 Lepidoptera larva, in addition to those listed above found on most species.

Sole sustainers of 19: Grey Shoulder-Knot Graptolitha ornitopus rhizolitha (young leaves), Lunar Marbled Brown Chaonia ruficornis / chaonia, Great Prominent Notodonta anceps / trepida, Small Black-Arches Nola strigula, Lesser Lutestring Asphalia diluta, Frosted Green Polyploca ridens, Oak Hook-Tip Drepana binaria / hamula, Merveille du Jour Griposia aprilina, Brindled Green Dryobotodes protea, Orange Upperwing Jodia croceago, Scarce Merveille du Jour Moma alpium / orion, Heart Dicycla oo, Dark Crimson Underwing Catocala sponsa, Light Crimson Underwing Catocala promissa, Lunar Double-Strife Minucia lunaris (young leaves only), Blotched Emerald Comibaena pustulata / bajularia, Brindled Pug Eupithecia abbreviata, Marbled Brown Drymonia dodonaea / trimacula, and Spring Usher Erannis leucophaearia.

One of two sustainers of 8: Large Marbled Tortrix Sarrothripus revayana other being Salix caprea, Scarce Silver-Lines Pseudoips prasinana / bicolorana / quercana other being Betula, Alchemist Catephia alchymista (in August) other being Ulmus, False Mocha Cosymbia punctaria other being Betula, Maiden's Blush Cosymbia punctaria other being Betula, Marbled Pug Eupithecia irriguata other being Fagus, Oak-tree Pug Eupithecia dodoneata other being Crataegus, and Brindled White Spot Ectropis extersaria / luridata other being Betula.

<u>One of three sustainers of 5</u>: Great Oak Beauty Boarmia roboraria others being Betula and Salix species, Purple Hairstreak Thecla quercus others being Castanea and Salix, Chestnut Conistra vaccinii others being other Quercus species and Ulmus, Common Fanfoot Herminia barbalis others being Alnus and Betula, and occasionally sustains Golden Rod Pug Eupithecia virgaureata (flowers) others being Dahlias, Senecio jacobea and Solidago.

Also sustains: Pale Oak Beauty Boarmia punctinalis / consortaria, Lobster Moth Stauropus fagi, Coxcomb Prominent Lophopteryx capucina / camelina, Common Lutestring Tethea duplaris, Scarce Vapourer Orgyia recens / gonostigma, Black V moth Leucoma v-nigrum / l-album, Pale Eggar Trichiura crataegii, December Moth Poecilo campapopuli, Least Black Arches Celama confusalis / cristulalis, Double Dart Graphiphora augur, Grey Arches Polia nebulosa (after hibernation), Pale-shouldered Brocade Hadena thalassina, Beautiful Brocade Hadena contigua, Small Quaker Orthosia cruda / pulverulenta, Common Quaker Orthosia stabilis, Twin-Spotted Quaker Orthosia munda, Clouded Drab Orthosia incerta / instabilis, Sprawler Brachyonycha sphinx / cassinia, Satellite Eupsilia transversa / satellitia, Dotted Chestnut Dasycampa rubiginea, Yellow-Line Quaker Agrochola macilenta, Flounced Chestnut Anchocelis helvola / rufina, Brown-Spot Pinion Anchocelis litura, Dark Chestnut Conistra ligula / spadicea, Miller Apatele leporina, Sycamore Apatele aceris, Dark Dagger Apatele tridens, Scarce Dagger Apatele auricoma, Copper Underwing Amphipyra pyramidea, Lunar-Spotted Pinion Cosmia pyralina, Green Silver-

Lines Bena fagana / prasinana, Nut-tree Tussock Colocasia coryli, Little Emerald Iodis lactaearia, Clay Triple-lines Cosymbia linearia / trilinearia, Broken-barred Carpet Electrophaeus corylata, Red-green Carpet Chloroclysta siterata / psittacata, Autumn Green Carpet Chloroclysta miata, Common White Wave Cabera pusaria, Barred Umber Anagoga pulveraria, August Thorn ennomos quercinaria / angularia, September Thorn Deuteronomos erosaria, Lunar Thorn Selenia lunaria, Scorched Wing Plagodis dolobraria, Scarce Umber Eriannis aurantiara, Small Brindled Beauty Apocheima hispidaria, Square-Spot Ectropis consonaria, Autumnal Moth Oporinia autumnata, November Moth Oporinia dilutata / nebulata, Common Emerald Hemithea aestivaria / strigata / thymiaria (after hibernation), Oak Eggar Bombyx / Lasiocampa quercus, and Bordered Sallow Pyrrhia umbra / marginata (flowers and seeds).

Suffers: Cabbage Moth Mamestra brassicae, Pebble Prominent Notodonta ziczac, Buff-Tip Phalera bucephala, Yellow / Gold Tail Euproctis similes / auriflua, Gipsy Moth Lymantria dispar, Black Arches Lymantria monacha, Hebrew Character Orthosia gothica, Pale Pinion Lithophane socia / petrificata, and Swordgrass Xylena exsoleta.

RANUNCULUS ACRIS, MEADOW BUTTERCUP

<u>Sole sustainer of</u> Slender-striped Rufous Coenocalpe lapidata.

Sustains: Lunar Yellow Underwing Triphaena orbona / subsequa, Beaded Chestnut Agrochola lychnidis / pistacina, and Fern Horisme tersata.

RANUNCULUS BULBOSUS, BULBOUS BUTTERCUP

Sustains: Beaded Chestnut Agrochola lychnidis / pistacina, and Flame Brocade Trigonophora flammea / empyrea.

RANUNCULUS FICARIA, LESSER CELANDINE

Sustains: Flame Brocade Trigonophora flammea / empyrea, and Twin-spot Carpet Colostygia didymata.

RANUNCULUS REPENS, CREEPING BUTTERCUP / CROWFOOT

Sustains: Lunar Yellow Underwing Triphaena orbona / subsequa, Flame Brocade Trigonophora flammea / empyrea, and Beaded Chestnut Agrochola lychnidis / pistacina.

RAPHANUS SATIVUS, RADISH

Suffers: Large White Pieris brassicae, and Small White P. rapae.

RESEDA ALBA, WHITE MIGNONETTE

Sustains Bath White Pontia daplidice.

Reseda lutea, WILD MIGNONETTE

Suffers: Large White Pieris brassicae, Bath White Pontia daplidice, and Small White P. rapae.

Reseda luteola, WELD / DYER'S ROCKET

Suffers: Bath White Pontia daplidice, Large White Pieris brassicae, and Small White P. rapae.

Rhamnus catharticus, BUCKTHORN

Flowers rich in nectar.

Sustains 7 Lepidoptera larva.

Sole sustainer of 2: Brown Scallop Philereme vetulata, and Dark Umber Philereme transversata / rhamnata.

One of two sustainers Brimstone Gonepteryx rhamni other being R. frangula.

One of three sustainers Tissue Triphosa dubitata others being Prunus padus and R. frangula.

Also sustains: Green Hairstreak Callophrys rubi (flowers and leaves), Lappet Gastropacha quercifolia, and Emperor Saturnia pavonia / carpini.

Rhamnus frangula, ALDER-BUCKTHORN

Flowers rich in nectar.

Sustains 8 Lepidoptera larva.

One of two sustainers Brimstone Gonepteryx rhamni other R. cathartica. One of three sustainers Tissue Triphosa dubitata others being Prunus padus and R. cathartica.

Also sustains: Lappet Gastropacha quercifolia, Emperor Saturnia pavonia / carpini, Yellow-barred Brindle Acasis viretata (flowers first, then green berries then leaves), Holly / Azure Blue Celastrina argiolus (flowers, flower buds, green berries and leaves), and suffers Emperor Saturnia pavonia / carpini.

RHEUM RHAPONTICUM, RHUBARB

Sustains Knotgrass moth Apatele rumicis.

RHINANTHUS CRISTA-GALLI, YELLOW RATTLE

Parasitic on grasses.

Sole sustainer of Grass Rivulet Perizoma albulata (in seed capsules).

One of three sustainers Lead-coloured Pug Eupithecia plumbeolata (flowers) others being Melampyrum species.

Also sustains Satyr Pug Eupithecia satyrata (flowers).

RHODODENDRONS

see also Azaleas and Ericaceae.

Sustains Alder Apatele alni.

RHYNCHOSPORA ALBA, WHITE BEAK-SEDGE

Sustains Large Heath / Marsh Ringlet Coenonympha tullia / davus / tiphon.

Ribes species

Sustain 15 Lepidoptera larva on most of the following species.

<u>One of three sustainers of 4</u>: Spinach Lygris mellinata / associata also on R. grossularia and R. nigrum, Phoenix Lygris prunata others being other Ribes species, Currant Pug Eupithecia assimilata others being other Ribes and Humulus, and Waved Umber Hemerophila abruptaria others being Ligustrum and Syringa.

Also sustains: Large Ranunculus Antitype flavicincta, Grey Chi moth Antitype chi, Copper Underwing Amphipyra pyramidea, Mamestra brassicae Cabbage Moth, Common Emerald Hemithea aestivaria / strigata / thymiaria (after hibernation), Garden Carpet moth Xanthorhoe fluctuata, Comma Polygonia c-album, Mottled Pug Eupithecia exiguata, V-moth Itama wauaria, and the Magpie Abraxas grossulariata which was once more common.

Suffers Currant Clearwing Sesia tipuliformis, the white with a brown head caterpillar bores in the stems which wilt and the fruit fails.

Ribes grossularia, GOOSEBERRY

<u>One of three sustainers</u> Phoenix Lygris prunata others being other Ribes species.

Also sustains: Comma Polygonia c-album, V-moth Itama wauaria, and suffers: Yellow / Gold Tail Euproctis similes / auriflua, Garden Carpet moth Xanthorhoe fluctuata. Magpie moth Abraxas grossulariata larvae overwinter in many places especially bark crevices and eat the foliage from early spring, this used to be widespread but seldom seen now.

RIBES NIGRUM BLACKCURRANTS

One of two sustainers Spinach Lygris mellinata / associata other being Ribes grossularia.

One of three sustainers of 2: Phoenix Lygris prunata others being other Ribes species, and Currant Pug Eupithecia assimilata others being other Ribes and Humulus.

Also sustains: Comma Polygonia c-album, Magpie Abraxas grossulariata, and V-moth Itama wauaria. Blackcurrants may host Looper caterpillars. Occasionally a Currant Clearwing moth / European Currant Borer Sesia tipuliformis caterpillar, whitish with brown head, may hollow out then live and pupate in the stems and branches often killing them. The adult is unusual in having no scales thus clear wings and so resembles a bee. This may be conflated with another or the same grub, the Blackcurrant Crown Borer Bembecia marginata, eggs are laid in summer, the larva overwinters at the base enters a cane, lives inside restricting growth and causing die back, after many months or years pupates then emerges as the Clearwing moth.

RIBES SANGUINEUM, FLOWERING CURRANT

Sustains: Magpie Abraxas grossulariata, and V-moth Itama wauaria.

ROBINIA PSEUDOACACIA, LOCUST / FALSE ACACIA

Flowers are rich in nectar.

Suffers Buff-Tip Phalera bucephala.

Rosa species, ROSES

Sustain 16 Lepidoptera larva: Small Quaker Orthosia cruda / pulverulenta, Brown-Spot Pinion Anchocelis litura, Common Emerald Hemithea aestivaria / strigata / thymiaria (after hibernation), Chevron Lygris testate, Autumn Green Carpet Chloroclysta miata, Small White Wave Asthena albulata / candidata, Lunar Thorn Selenia lunaria, Little Thorn Cepphis advenaria, occasionally Elephant Hawkmoth Deilephila elpenor, suffer Scarce Vapourer Orgyia recens / gonostigma. Yellow / Gold Tail Euproctis similes / auriflua, Cream-spot Tiger Arctia villica, Jersey Tiger Euplagia quadripunctaria / hera, Dun-Bar Cosmia trapezina, Grey Dagger Apatele psi, and Copper Underwing Amphipyra pyramidea.

Rosa arvensis, FIELD ROSE and R. canina, DOG ROSE

These have similar co-lives. Sustain 9 Lepidoptera larva.

One of two sustainers of 3: Shoulder-stripe Earophila badiata other being R. spinosissima, Streamer Anticlea derivata / nigrofasciaria other being Lonicera, and Barred Yellow Cidaria fulvata other being R. spinosissima (and occasionally garden varieties).

Also sustains: Lobster Moth Stauropus fagi, Brown Tail Euproctis chrysorrhoea / phaecorrhoea, Dotted Clay Amathes baia, Red-green Carpet Chloroclysta siterata / psittacata, November Moth Oporinia dilutata / nebulata, and Hedge Dagger Acronycta psi.

Rosa spinosissima, BURNET ROSE.

One of two sustainers of 2: Shoulder-stripe Earophila badiata, and Barred Yellow Cidaria fulvata others of both being R. canina rose and occasionally garden varieties.

Also sustains: Fox Moth Macrothylacia rubi, Knotgrass moth Apatele rumicis.

RUBIA PEREGRINA, WILD MADDER

<u>One of three sustainers</u> Hummingbird Hawkmoth Macroglossum stellatarum others being Galium species.

RUBUS CAESIUS, DEWBERRY

Sustains: Buff Arches Habrosyne pyritoides / derasa, Kent Black-Arches Nola albula / albulalis, and Beautiful Carpet Mesoleuca albicillata.

RUBUS FRUTICOSUS, BLACKBERRIES
PLUS LOGANBERRIES and other HYBRIDS

Sustain 44 Lepidoptera larva.

<u>Sole sustainer of</u> Peach Blossom Thyatira batis.

<u>One of three sustainers</u> Scarce Footman Eilema complana(algae and leaves) others being Abies and Prunus spinosa.

Also sustains: Grizzled Skipper Pyrgus malvae / alveolus, Buff Arches Habrosyne pyritoides / derasa, Scarce Vapourer Orgyia recens / gonostigma, Brown Tail Euproctis chrysorrhoea / phaecorrhoea, Oak Eggar Lasiocampa quercus, Grass Eggar Lasiocampa trifolii, Fox Moth Macrothylacia / Bombyx rubi, Emperor Saturnia pavonia / carpini, Dotted Clay Amathes baia, Six-striped Rustic Amathes sexstrigata / umbrosa, Green Arches Anaplectoides prasina / herbida, Powdered Quaker Orthosia gracilis, Brown-Spot Pinion Anchocelis litura, Light Knotgrass Apatele menyanthidis, Scarce Dagger Apatele auricoma, Saxon

Hyppa rectilinear, Small Grass Emerald Chlorissa viridata, Beautiful Carpet Mesoleuca albicillata, Hedge Dagger Acronycta psi, Common Pug Eupithecia vulgata, occasionally Blossom Underwing Orthosia miniosa, and Portland Ribbon Wave Sterrha degeneraria, possibly Dotted-Border Wave Sterrha sylvestraria / straminata, V Pug Chloroclystis coronata (flowers), Rosy Marbled Hapalotis venustula (flowers), Holly / Azure Blue Celastrina argiolus (in autumn)(flowers, flower buds, green berries and leaves), and Green Hairstreak Callophrys rubi (flowers and leaves).

In spring, after hibernation, brambles sustain some Lepidoptera larva that were sustained by other plants the previous autumn: Purple Clay Diarsia brunnea, Ingrailed Clay Diarsia festiva / primulae, Triple-spotted Clay Amathes ditrapezium, Silvery Arches Polia hepatica / tincta, Double Square-spot Amathes triangulum, Great Brocade Eurois occulta, Grey Arches Polia nebulosa, Early Thorn Selenia bilunaria / illunaria, Little Thorn Cepphis advenaria.

Suffers: Jersey Tiger Euplagia quadripunctaria / hera, Scarlet Tiger Panaxia dominula, Pale Pinion Lithophane socia / petrificata, and Beautiful Arches Eumichtus satura. Yellow / Gold Tail Euproctis similes / auriflua, on it's fruits, and a Tortrix caterpillar, Bramble Shoot Webber Notocelia uddmanniana, first whitish then brownish red with a black head, webs the leaves together and destroys the ends of shoots.

RUBUS IDAEUS, RASPBERRY
Sustains 18 Lepidoptera larva.

Sole sustainer Small Fanfoot Zanclognatha grisealis / nemoralis.

Fanfoot Zanclognatha tarsipennalis others being Hedera and Salix caprea, and Sharp-angled Carpet Euphyia unangulata others being Alsine and Stellaria.

Also sustains: Pale Oak Beauty Boarmia punctinalis / consortaria, Silver Washed Fritillary Argynnis paphia, Grizzled Skipper Pyrgus malvae / alveolus, Buff Arches Habrosyne pyritoides / derasa, Emperor Saturnia pavonia / carpini, Kent Black-Arches Nola albula / albulalis, Beautiful Arches Eumichtus satura, Scarce Dagger Apatele auricoma, Saxon Hyppa rectilinear, Beautiful Carpet Mesoleuca albicillata, Common Pug Eupithecia vulgata, and Early Thorn Selenia bilunaria / illunaria.

Suffers: Raspberry Cane / Crown Borer Bembecia hylaeiformi, eggs are laid in summer, the larva overwinters at the base enters a cane, lives inside restricting growth and causing die back, after up to several years it pupates then emerges as a clearwing moth about an inch long with four yellow bands on its abdomen so looks like a wasp. Raspberry moth Lampronia rubiella, reddish grub also tunnels and causes withered wilted shoots in spring, may also damage the plug of the fruit, hibernates in debris.

Also suffers: caterpillars that bother apples, see Malus, may also visit raspberries: Vapourer moth, the Tortrix moth, and Bud moth.

RUDBECKIA SPECIES, CONEFLOWERS

Suffers: Tortrix moth, and Swift moth white caterpillars eating their roots.

Rumex, DOCKS & SORRELS
Sustain 20 plus Lepidoptera larva.

One of two sustainers of 2: Cyclamen tortrix Clepsis spectrana other being Urtica dioica, and Bird's-Wing Dipterygia scabriuscula / pinastri other being Polygonum arvense.

Also sustains: Striped Hawkmoth Celerio livornica, Autumnal Rustic Amathes glareosa, Great Brocade Eurois occulta, Lesser Yellow Underwing Triphaena comes / orbona, Lesser Broad-border Triphaena lanthina, Broad-bordered Yellow Underwing Lampra fimbriata / fimbria, Feathered Ranunculus Eumichtis lichenea, Uncertain Caradrina alsines, Blood-vein Timandra griseata / Calothysanis amata / amataria, Gem moth Nycterosea obstipata / fluviata / gemmata, Yellow Shell Camptogramma / Euphyia bilineata, Black-veined Moth Siona lineata / dealbata, Forester moths Adscita statices, Tiger moths Arctia caia and A. villica, Buff Ermine Spilosoma lutea, Cnephasia interjectana, Silver Y moth Autographa gamma, Angle shades Phlogophora meticulosa, Turnip moth Agrotis segetum, and Olethreutes lacunana.

Rumex SPECIES BUT NOT SORRELS
Sustain 45 Lepidoptera larva.

Sole sustainers of Grey Arches Polia nebulosa (may eat other plants after hibernation).

One of three sustainers of 6: Light Feathered Rustic Agrotis cinerea others being Taraxacum and Thymus, Shuttle-Shaped Dart Agrotis puta / radius others being Polygonum arvense and Taraxacum, Dog's Tooth Hadena suasa / dissimillis others being Plantago major and Polygonum arvense, Stout Dart Spaelotis ravida / obscura others being Leontodon and Taraxacum, Small

Square-spot Diarsia rubi / bella others being Taraxacum and Stellaria, Rustic Caradrina blanda /taraxaci others being Plantago species and Stellaria chickweeds, and Shoulder-striped Wainscot Leucania comma others being Dactylis glomerata and Rumex species.

Also sustains: Cabbage Moth Mamestra brassicae Ghost / Otter moth Hepialus lupuli, Muslin moth Diaphora / Cycnia / mendica, Ruby Tiger Phragmatobia fuliginosa, Heart and Dart Agrotis exclamationis, Dotted Rustic Rhyacia simulans / pyrophila, Double Dart Graphiphora augur, Purple Clay Diarsia brunnea, Ingrailed Clay Diarsia festiva / primulae, Flame Shoulder Ochropleura plecta, Dotted Clay Amathes baia, Triple-spotted Clay Amathes ditrapezium, Square-spotted Clay Amathes stigmatica / rhomboides, Six-striped Rustic Amathes sexstrigata / umbrosa, Square-spot Rustic Amathes xanthographa, Flame Axylia putris, Green Arches Anaplectoides prasina / herbida, Red Chestnut Cerastis rubricosa, Gothic Phalaena typica (after hibernation), Silvery Arches Polia hepatica / tincta, Brown Brocade / Bright-line Brown Eye Lacanobia oleracea / Diataraxia oleracea, Pale-shouldered Brocade Hadena thalassina. Hebrew Character Orthosia gothica, Orange Wainscot (Brown-line Bright-eye) Leucania conigera, Deep Brown Dart Aporophyla lutulenta, Beaded Chestnut Agrochola lychnidis / pistacina, Clouded Brindle Apamea characterea / hepatica, Rosy Rustic Hydraecia micacea, Common Emerald Hemithea aestivaria / strigata / thymiaria, Isle of Wight Wave Sterrha humiliata / osseata, Plain Wave Idaea straminata / Sterrha inornata, Riband Wave Sterrha aversata, Cream Wave Scopula floslactata / remutata / remutaria, Silver-ground Carpet Xanthorhoe montanata, Green Carpet Colostygia pectinataria / viridaria, Belted Beauty Nyssia zonaria, and Garden Tiger Arctia caia.

Rumex acetosa, SORREL

Sustains: Brown-Spot Pinion Anchocelis litura, Sweet-Gale Apatele euphorbiae / myricae, Knotgrass moth Apatele rumicis, Small Copper Lycaena phlaeus, and Plain Clay Amathes depuncta.

Rumex acetosella, SHEEP'S SORREL

One of three sustainers Shoulder-striped Wainscot Leucania comma others being Dactylis glomerata and Rumex species.

Also sustains: Small Copper Lycaena phlaeus, Ashworth's Rustic Amathes ashworthii, Black Rustic Aporophyla nigra, and Clouded Buff Diacrisia sannio / russula.

Rumex crispus, CURLED DOCK

Sustains: Barred Chestnut Diarsia dahlii, Plain Clay Amathes depuncta, and Small Mottled Willow Laphygma exigua.

Rumex hydrolapathum, GREAT WATER-DOCK

One of two sustainers Large Copper Lycaena dispar dispar (became extinct in 1865), re-introductions of European L. dispar batuvus and L. dispar rutilus attempted, other sustainer being R. obtusifolius.

Also sustains Water Ermine Spilosoma urticae / papyratia.

Rumex obtusifolius, BROAD-LEAVED DOCK

Sustains 11 Lepidoptera larva.

Other of two sustainers Large Copper Lycaena dispar dispar other being R. hydrolapathum.

Also sustains: Ghost / Otter Moth Hepialus lupuli, Heart And Club Agrotis clavis / corticea, Pearly Underwing Peridroma porphyrea / saucia, Setaceous Hebrew Character Amathes e-nigrum, Double Square-spot Amathes triangulum, Knotgrass moth Apatele rumicis, Small Copper Lycaena phlaeus, Black Rustic Aporophyla nigra, Clouded Buff Diacrisia sannio / russula, and Water Ermine Spilosoma urticae / papyratia.

Rumex pulcher, FIDDLE DOCK

Sustains: Small Copper Lycaena phlaeus, Black Rustic Aporophyla nigra, and Barred Chestnut Diarsia dahlii.

Ruscus aculeatus, BUTCHER'S BROOM

Sustains Mottled Beauty Alcis repandata.

Salix, WILLOWS & SALLOWS

Sustain 65 Lepidoptera larva on almost all species.

One of three sustainers of 3: Great Oak Beauty Boarmia roboraria others being Betula and Quercus species, Purple Hairstreak Thecla quercus others being Castanea and Quercus species, and Suspected Parastichtis suspecta others being Betula and Populus nigra.

Also sustains: Pale Oak Beauty Boarmia punctinalis / consortaria, Small Chocolate-tip Clostera pigra / reclusa, Grass Eggar Lasiocampa trifolii, Pebble Prominent Nodonta ziczac, Buff-Tip Phalera bucephala, Buff Tiger Nemeophila russula, Silver-Studded Blue Phlebius argus / aegon, Privet Hawkmoth Sphinx ligustri, Yellow / Gold Tail Euproctis similes / auriflua, Sprawler Brachyonycha sphinx / cassinia, Golden-rod Brindle Lithomoia solidaginis, Pale Eggar Trichiura crataegii, Emperor Saturnia pavonia / carpini, Barred Chestnut Diarsia dahlii, Triple-spotted Clay Amathes ditrapezium, White-marked Gypsitea leucographa, Red Chestnut Cerastis rubricosa, Black Arches Lymantria monacha, Silvery Arches Polia hepatica / tincta (in spring), Small Quaker Orthosia cruda / pulverulenta, Common Quaker Orthosia stabilis. Twin-Spotted Quaker Orthosia munda, Flounced Chestnut Anchocelis helvola / rufina, Brown-Spot Pinion Anchocelis litura, Dark Chestnut Conistra ligula / spadicea, Miller Apatele leporina, Grey Dagger Apatele psi, Old Lady Mormo maura, Autumn Green Carpet Chloroclysta miata, Dark Marbled Carpet Dysstroma citrata / immanata, May Highflyer Hydriomena coerulata / impluviata / trifasciata, Mottled Pug Eupithecia exiguata, Common Pug Eupithecia vulgata, Autumnal Moth Oporinia autumnata, November Moth

Oporinia dilutata / nebulata, Waved Carpet Hydrelia testaceata / sylvata, Magpie Abraxas grossulariata, Common White Wave Cabera pusaria, Scorched Wing Plagodis dolobraria, Little Thorn Cepphis advenaria, Bordered Sallow Pyrrhia umbra / marginata (eats flowers and seeds), Dingy Footman Eilema griseola (on lichens on wood) Dotted Footman Pelosia muscerda (on algae on wood), Goat Moth Cossus ligniperda (on live and dead wood), and occasionally Small Angle-Shades Euplexia lucipara, Mottled Rustic Caradrina morpheus, and Cabbage Moth Mamestra brassicae.

Willows and Sallows may also be secondary food source for yet more after hibernation; thus in spring foliage sustains: Double Square-spot Amathes triangulum, Great Brocade Eurois occulta, Lesser Yellow Underwing Triphaena comes / orbona, Lesser Broad-border Triphaena lanthina, Least Yellow Underwing Triphaena interjecta, Broad-bordered Yellow Underwing Lampra fimbriata / fimbria, Green Arches Anaplectoides prasina / herbida, Gothic Phalaena typica. Their catkins attract if not sustain the Yellow-Horned Moth Asphalia / Achlya flavicornis, and Dark Swordgrass Agrotis suffusa / ipsilon.

Suffer: Gipsy Moth Lymantria dispar, Hebrew Character Orthosia gothica, Pale Pinion Lithophane socia / petrificata, Beautiful Arches Eumichtus satura, and Grey Chi moth Antitype chi.

Salix alba, WHITE WILLOW
Sustains 34 Lepidoptera larva in addition to 65 Lepidoptera larva on almost all species.

One of two sustainers of 2: Small Seraphim Mysticoptera sexalata / sexalisata other being Salix caprea, and Dingy Shears Apamea ypsillon / fissipuncta other being Populus nigra.

: Rosy Marsh Coenophila subrosea others being Myrica gale and Salix repens, and Cream-Bordered Green Pea Earias clorana others being Salix triandra and Salix viminalis.

Also sustains: Satellite Eupsilia transversa / satellitia, Mouse Amphipyra tragopogonis, Lappet Gastropacha quercifolia, Pale Shining Brown Polia nitens / advena, Eyed Hawkmoth Smerinthus ocellata, Pussmoth Cerura vinula, Sallow Kitten Harpyia furcula, Small Chocolate-tip Clostera pigra / reclusa and occassionally Lobster Moth Stauropus fagi, Red-line Quaker Agrochola lota, Swallow Prominent Pheosia tremula / dictaea, Large Tortoiseshell Nymphalis polychloros, Camberwell Beauty Nymphalis antiopa, Eyed Hawkmoth Smerinthus ocellata, Clouded Drab Orthosia incerta / instabilis, Powdered Quaker Orthosia gracilis, Scarce Vapourer Orgyia recens / gonostigma, Pale Prominent Pterostoma palpina, White Satin Leucoma salicis, Copper Underwing Amphipyra pyramidea, Glaucous Shears Hadena bombycina / glauca, Minor Shoulder-knot Bombycia viminalis, Double Kidney Zenobia retusa, Red Underwing Catocala nupta, Herald Scoliopteryx libatrix, Lesser Belle Colobochyla salicalis, July Highflyer Hydriomena furcata / elutata / sordidata, Ruddy Highflyer Hydriomena ruberata, Clouded Border Lomaspilis marginata, and Bordered Beuaty Epione repandaria / apiciaria

Salix atrocinerea, GREY SALLOW
Sustains 53 Lepidoptera larva in addition to 65 Lepidoptera larva on almost all species.

One of two sustainers Pink-Barred Sallow Citria lutea / flavago / silago (catkins at first) other being Salix caprea.

<u>One of three sustainers of 5</u>: Neglected / Grey Rustic Amathes castanea / neglecta others being Erica cinerea and Salix caprea, Sallow Moth Cirrhia icteritia/ fulvago / cerago others being Populus nigra and Salix caprea, Dingy Mocha Cosymbia pendularia / orbicularia others being Alnus and Salix caprea, Slender Pug Eupithecia tenuiata others being Salix aurita and Salix caprea, and Peacock Moth Semiothisa notata others being Betula and Salix caprea.

Also sustains: Lappet Gastropacha quercifolia, Pale Shining Brown Polia nitens / advena, Iron Prominent Notodonta dromedaries, Small Eggar Eriogaster lanestris, Square-spot Rustic Amathes xanthographa (in spring), Brown Brocade / Bright-line Brown Eye Diataraxia oleracea, Pale-shouldered Brocade Hadena thalassina, Sweet-Gale Apatele euphorbiae / myricae, Eyed Hawkmoth Smerinthus ocellata, Pussmoth Cerura vinula, Sallow Kitten Harpyia furcula, Small Chocolate-tip Clostera pigra / reclusa, Red-line Quaker Agrochola lota, Large Tortoiseshell Nymphalis polychloros, Camberwell Beauty Nymphalis antiopa, Eyed Hawkmoth Smerinthus ocellata, Coxcomb Prominent Lophopteryx capucina / camelina, Purple Emperor Apatura iris, Chocolate-Tip Clostera curtula, Ingrailed Clay Diarsia festiva / primulae (in spring), Dotted Clay Amathes baia (in spring), Dark Dagger Apatele tridens, Dark Tussock Dasychira fascelina, Purple Clay Diarsia brunnea (in spring), Scarce Vapourer Orgyia recens / gonostigma, Pale Prominent Pterostoma palpina, White Satin Leucoma salicis, Copper Underwing Amphipyra pyramidea, Glaucous Shears Hadena bombycina / glauca, Northern Drab Orthosia advena / opima, Double Dart Graphiphora augur (in spring), Minor Shoulder-knot Bombycia viminalis, Double Kidney Zenobia retusa, Herald Scoliopteryx libatrix, Lesser Belle Colobochyla salicalis, Little

Emerald Iodis lactaearia, Chevron Lygris testate, Northern Spinach Lygris populata, Common Marbled Carpet Dysstroma truncata / russata/ centumnotata, July Highflyer Hydriomena furcata / elutata / sordidata, Ruddy Highflyer Hydriomena ruberata, Scallop Shell Calocalpe undulata, Seraphim Lobophora halterata / hexapterata, Clouded Border Lomaspilis marginata, Common Wave Cabera exanthemata, Barred Umber Anagoga pulveraria, and occasionally Lobster Moth Stauropus fagi.

Salix aurita, ROUND-EARED / EARED WILLOW

Sustains 14 Lepidoptera larva in addition to 65 Lepidoptera larva on almost all species.

One of three sustainers of 2: Slender Pug Eupithecia tenuiata others being Salix atrocinerea and Salix caprea, and Netted Mountain-Moth Isturgia carbonaria others being Arctostaphylos and Betula.

Also sustains: Sweet-Gale Apatele euphorbiae / myricae, Light Knotgrass Apatele menyanthidis, Eyed Hawkmoth Smerinthus ocellata, Pussmoth Cerura vinula, Sallow Kitten Harpyia furcula, Small Chocolate-tip Clostera pigra / reclusa, Red-line Quaker Agrochola lota, Northern Drab Orthosia advena / opima, July Highflyer Hydriomena furcata / elutata / sordidata, Ruddy Highflyer Hydriomena ruberata, Common Heath-moth Ematurga atomaria, and occassionally Lobster Moth Stauropus fagi.

Salix caprea, GOAT WILLOW

Sustains 65 Lepidoptera larva in addition to 65 Lepidoptera larva on almost all species.

One of two sustainers of 5: Scarce Chocolate-tip Clostera anachoreta other being Populus nigra, Pink-Barred Sallow Citria lutea / flavago / silago(catkins first) other being Salix atrocinerea, Large Marbled Tortrix Sarrothripus revayana other being Quercus species, and Small Seraphim Mysticoptera sexalata / sexalisata other being Salix alba.

One of three sustainers of 8: Chestnut Conistra vaccinii others being Quercus robur and Ulmus campestris, Neglected / Grey Rustic Amathes castanea / neglecta others being Erica cinerea and Salix atrocinerea, Sallow Moth Cirrhia icteritia / fulvago / cerago others being Populus nigra and Salix atrocinerea, Dingy Mocha Cosymbia pendularia / orbicularia others being Alnus and Salix atrocinerea, Fanfoot Zanclognatha tarsipennalis others being Hedera and Rubus idaeus, Slender Pug Eupithecia tenuiata others being Salix aurita and Salix atrocinerea, Peacock Moth Semiothisa notata others being Betula and Salix alba, and Sharp-angled Peacock Semiothisa alternaria / alternata others being Alnus and Prunus spinosa.

Also sustains: Eyed Hawkmoth Smerinthus ocellata, Pussmoth Cerura vinula, Sallow Kitten Harpyia furcula, Small Chocolate-tip Clostera pigra, Square-spotted Clay Amathes stigmatica / rhomboides, Grey Arches Polia nebulosa, Dark Brocade Eumichtis adusta, Poplar Grey Apatele megacephala, Mouse Amphipyra tragopogonis, Red-line Quaker Agrochola lota, Large Tortoiseshell Nymphalis polychloros, Camberwell Beauty Nymphalis antiopa, Eyed Hawkmoth Smerinthus ocellata, Clouded Drab Orthosia incerta / instabilis, Powdered Quaker Orthosia gracilis, Coxcomb Prominent Lophopteryx capucina / camelina, Purple Emperor Apatura iris, Chocolate-Tip Clostera curtula, Ingrailed Clay Diarsia festiva / primulae (in spring), Dotted Clay Amathes baia (in spring), Dark Dagger Apatele tridens; Dark Tussock Dasychira fascelina, Purple Clay Diarsia brunnea (in spring), Scarce Vapourer Orgyia recens / gonostigma, Pale Prominent Pterostoma palpina, White Satin

Leucoma salicis, Copper Underwing Amphipyra pyramidea, Glaucous Shears Hadena bombycina / glauca, Northern Drab Orthosia advena / opima, Double Dart Graphiphora augur (in spring), Minor Shoulder-knot Bombycia viminalis, Saxon Hyppa rectilinear, Double Kidney Zenobia retusa, Herald Scoliopteryx libatrix, Lesser Belle Colobochyla salicalis, Chevron Lygris testate, Northern Spinach Lygris populata, Common Marbled Carpet Dysstroma truncata / russata / centumnotata, July Highflyer Hydriomena furcata / elutata / sordidata, Ruddy Highflyer Hydriomena ruberata, Scallop Shell Calocalpe undulata, Seraphim Lobophora halterata / hexapterata, Early Tooth-striped Nothopteryx carpinata / lobulata, Pale November Moth Oporinia christyi, Clouded Border Lomaspilis marginata, Common Wave Cabera exanthemata, Barred Umber Anagoga pulveraria, Canary-shouldered Thorn Deuteronomos alniaria / tiliaria, Brick Agrochola circellaris / ferruginea (catkins and buds), Scarce Umber Eriannis aurantiara, and occassionally Lobster Moth Stauropus fagi.

Salix fragilis, CRACK-WILLOW
Sustain 65 Lepidoptera larva found on almost all species and

One of three sustainers: Dingy Shears Apamea pysillon / fissipuncta others being other Salix species and Populus nigra.

Also sustains: Red-line Quaker Agrochola lota, and Red Underwing Catocala nupta.

Salix phylicifolia, TEA-LEAVED WILLOW
Sustain 65 Lepidoptera larva found on almost all species and

Sustains Dark Bordered Beauty Epione vespertaria / parallelaria.

SALIX PURPUREA, **PURPLE WILLOW**

Sustain 65 Lepidoptera larva found on almost all species and

Sustains Swallow Prominent Pheosia tremula / dictaea.

SALIX REPENS, **CREEPING WILLOW**

Sustains 17 Lepidoptera larva in addition to 65 Lepidoptera larva on almost all species.

One of two sustainers Smoky Wave Scopula ternata / fumata other being Vaccinium myrtillus.

One of three sustainers of 2: Rosy Marsh Coenophila subrosea others being Myrica gale and Salix alba, and Nonconformist Graptolitha lamda others being Myrica gale and Vaccinium uliginosum.

Also sustains: Light Knotgrass Apatele menyanthidis, Fox Moth Macrothylacia rubi, Portland Moth Actebia praecox, Ashworth's Rustic Amathes ashworthii, Autumnal Rustic Amathes glareosa, Sweet-Gale Apatele euphorbiae / myricae, Dark Tussock Dasychira fascelina, Purple Clay Diarsia brunnea (in spring), Glaucous Shears Hadena bombycina / glauca, Northern Drab Orthosia advena / opima, Grey Mountain Carpet Entephria caesiata, Northern Argent and Sable Eulype subhastata, Bordered Beauty Epione repandaria / apiciaria, and Dark Bordered Beauty Epione vespertaria / parallelaria.

SALIX TRIANDRA, **FRENCH / ALMOND WILLOW**

Sustain 65 Lepidoptera larva found on almost all species and

One of three sustainers Cream-Bordered Green Pea Earias clorana others being Salix alba and Salix viminalis.

Salix viminalis, OSIER

Sustains 12 Lepidoptera larva in addition to 65 Lepidoptera larva on almost all species.

One of three sustainers Cream-Bordered Green Pea Earias clorana others being Salix alba and Salix repens.

Also sustains: Knotgrass Apatele rumicis, Large Tortoiseshell Nymphalis polychloros, Camberwell Beauty Nymphalis antiopa, Eyed Hawkmoth Smerinthus ocellata, Northern Drab Orthosia advena / opima, Double Dart Graphiphora augur (in spring), Minor Shoulder-knot Bombycia viminalis, Double Kidney Zenobia retusa, Herald Scoliopteryx libatrix, Clouded Border Lomaspilis marginata, and Scarce Umber Eriannis aurantiara.

Salsola kali, PRICKLY SALTWORT

Sustains: Diamond-back moth Plutella maculipennis, and Sand Dart Agrotis ripae.

Salvia officinalis, SAGE

Sustains: Grey Chi moth Antitype chi, and Bordered Straw Heliothis peltigera (eats mostly flowers and seeds).

Sambucus nigra, ELDERBERRY

Sustains: Swallow-tailed moth Ourapteryx sambucaria, and occasionally Frosted Orange Gortyna flavago / ochracea (in stems).

Saponaria officinalis, SOAPWORT

Flowers are accessible to Lepidoptera only.

Sarothamnus / Cytisus scoparius / scoparia, BROOM

Sustains 29 Lepidoptera larva.

Sole sustainer of 4: June Belle Ortholitha umbrifera, Streak Chesias legatella / spartiata, Broom-tip Chesias rufata / obliquaria, and Frosted Yellow Isturgia limbaria / conspicuata.

One of two sustainers Rest-Harrow Aplasta ononaria other being Ononis arvensis.

One of three sustainers of 2: Grass Emerald Pseudoterpna pruinata / cytisariaothers being Genista and Ulex, and Bordered Grey Selidosema plumaria / ericetaria others being Calluna vulgaris and Trifoliums.

Also sustains: Silver-Studded Blue Phlebius, Dark Tussock Dasychira fascelina, Grass Eggar Lasiocampa trifolii, Feathered Footman Coscinia striata / grammica, Autumnal Rustic Amathes glareosa, Lesser Yellow Underwing Triphaena comes / orbona (after hibernation), Pale Shining Brown Polia nitens / advena, Light Brocade Hadena w-latinum / genistae, Pale-shouldered Brocade Hadena thalassina, Flame Brocade Trigonophora flammea / empyrea (only in last instar), Dun-Bar Cosmia trapezina, Large Emerald Geometra papilionaria, Small Scallop Sterrha emarginata, Lead Belle Ortholitha mucronata / plumbaria / palumbaria, Scalloped Hazel Gonodontis bidentata, Orange Moth Angerona prunaria, Willow Beauty Alcis rhomboidaria / gemmaria, Scotch Annulet Gnophos myrtillata / obfuscaria, Grass Wave Perconia strigillaria, Long Tailed Blue

Lampides boeticus (flowers and seeds), Holly / Azure Blue Celastrina argiolus (flowers, flower buds, green berries and leaves), and Green Hairstreak Callophrys rubi (flowers and leaves).

SAXIFRAGA AIZOIDES, YELLOW SAXIFRAGE
Flowers rich in nectar.

One of three sustainers Small Autumnal / Carpet Oporinia filigrammaria others being Erica species and Vaccinium myrtillus.

Also sustains: Northern Rustic Ammogrotis lucernea, Red Carpet moth Xanthorhoe munitata, Grey Mountain Carpet Entephria caesiata, and Yellow-ringed Carpet Entephria flavicinctata / ruficinctata.

SAXIFRAGA HYPNOIDES, MOSSY SAXIFRAGE
Flowers rich in nectar.

Sustains: Northern Rustic Ammogrotis lucernea, and Yellow-ringed Carpet Entephria flavicinctata / ruficinctata.

SAXIFRAGA GRANULATA, MEADOW SAXIFRAGE
Flowers rich in nectar.

Sustains: Northern Rustic Ammogrotis lucernea,Yellow-ringed Carpet Entephria flavicinctata / ruficinctata, Lime-speck Pug Eupithecia centaureata / oblongata (eats flowers), and Wormwood Pug Eupithecia absinthiata / minutata.

SAXIFRAGA NIVALIS, ALPINE / ARCTIC SAXIFRAGE
Flowers rich in nectar.

Sustains: Twin-spot Carpet Colostygia didymata (flowers), and Northern Rustic Ammogrotis lucernea.

Saxifraga oppositifolia, PURPLE / MOUNTAIN SAXIFRAGE

Flowers rich in nectar.

Sustains: Northern Rustic Ammogrotis lucernea, and Yellow-ringed Carpet Entephria flavicinctata / ruficinctata.

Scabiosa arvensis, FIELD SCABIOUS

Flowers rich in nectar.

Sustains 7 Lepidoptera larva.

One of two sustainers Narrow-bordered Bee-Hawkmoth Hemaris tityus bombyliformis / Macroglossa fuciformis other being **S.** succissa.

Also sustains: Deep Brown Dart Aporophyla lutulenta, Feathered Ranunculus Eumichtis lichenea, Marbled Clover Heliothis dipsacea / viriplaca (flowers and seeds), Shaded Pug Eupithecia subumbrata / scabiosata (flowers), Satyr Pug Eupithecia satyrata (flowers), and possibly Portland Ribbon Wave Sterrha degeneraria.

Scabiosa columbaria, LESSER / SMALL SCABIOUS

Flowers rich in nectar.

Sustains: Lime-speck Pug Eupithecia centaureata / oblongata (flowers), Wormwood Pug Eupithecia absinthiata / minutata, Satyr Pug Eupithecia satyrata (flowers), and possibly Portland Ribbon Wave Sterrha degeneraria.

SCABIOSA SUCCISSA, DEVIL'S-BIT SCABIOUS

Flowers rich in nectar.

Sustains 8 Lepidoptera larva.

<u>One of two sustainers</u> Narrow-bordered Bee-Hawkmoth Hemaris tityus / bombyliformis other being **S.** arvensis.

Also sustains: Marsh / Greasy Fritillary Euphydryas aurinia / artemis, Striped Hawkmoth Celerio livornica, Clouded Buff Diacrisia sannio / russula, Feathered Ranunculus Eumichtis lichenea, Marbled Clover Heliothis dipsacea / viriplaca (flowers and seeds), Satyr Pug Eupithecia satyrata (flowers), and possibly Portland Ribbon Wave Sterrha degeneraria.

SCILLA NONSCRIPTA, BLUEBELL

Sustains: Autumnal Rustic Amathes glareosa, and Six-striped Rustic Amathes sexstrigata / umbrosa.

SCIRPUS CAESPITOSUS, TUFTED DEER'S-GRASS

Sustains: Antler Cerapteryx graminis, Confused Apammea furva, and Slender Brindle Apamea scolopacina.

SCIRPUS LACUSTRIS, BULRUSH

Sustains: Reed Wainscot Nonagria algae / cannae (in stem), and Webb's Wainscot Nonagria sparganii (in stem).

SCIRPUS MARITIMUS, SEA CLUB-RUSH

<u>Sole sustainer of</u> Saltern Ear-Moth Hydraecia paludis (in roots).

SCIRPUS PALUSTRIS, CREEPING CLUB-RUSH

Sustains White Point Leucania albipuncta.

SCROPHULARIA AQUATICA, WATER FIGWORT / BETONY

<u>One of two sustainers</u> Water Betony Cucullia scrophulariae (flowers and seeds) other **S.** nodosa.

Also sustains: Six-striped Rustic Amathes sexstrigata / umbrosa, Mullein Shark Cucullia verbasci, and Frosted Orange Gortyna flavago /ochracea (in stems).

SCROPHULARIA NODOSA, COMMON / KNOTTED FIGWORT

<u>One of two sustainers</u> Water Betony Cucullia scrophulariae(flowers and seeds) other S. aquatica.

Also sustains: Mullein Shark Cucullia verbasci, and Frosted Orange Gortyna flavago / ochracea (in stems).

SCROPHULARIA VERNALIS, YELLOW FIGWORT

Sustains Purple Clay Diarsia brunnea.

SECALE CEREALE, RYE

Sustains: White-line Dart Euoxa tritici / aquiline (young plants), Rosy Minor Procus literosa (in stems), and Brighton Wainscot Oria musculosa (in stems).

SEDUM ACRE, BITING STONECROP

Flowers rich in nectar.

Sustains: Northern Rustic Ammogrotis lucernea, Feathered Ranunculus Eumichtis lichenea, and Yellow-ringed Carpet Entephria flavicinctata / ruficinctata.

Sedum album, WHITE STONECROP

Sustains Mullein Wave Scopula marginepunctata / promutata / incanata.

Sedum telephium, ORPINE

Flowers rich in nectar.
Sustains Common Pug Eupithecia vulgata.

Senecio erucifolius, NARROW-LEAVED RAGWORT

Sustains: Lime-speck Pug Eupithecia centaureata / oblongata (flowers), and Wormwood Pug Eupithecia absinthiata / minutata.

Senecio jacobaea, RAGWORT / RAGWEED

One observer saw blooms visited by 49 different species mostly bees and flies, another reference gives 40 species; 3 butterflies and moths, 16 species bee, 18 species flies and 3 other.

Blooms themselves are particularly attractive to some Lepidoptera adults: Ear Moth Hydraecia nictitans, Rosy Rustic Hydraecia micacea, Antler / Grass Moth Cerapteryx / Charaeus graminis, White-Line Dart Agrotis tritici, Portland Moth Arotis praecox, and Lesser Narrow-Bordered Yellow Underwing Triphaena comes / orbona.

Sustains 15 Lepidoptera larva on foliage and other parts.

One of three sustainers Golden Rod Pug Eupithecia virgaureata (eats flowers) occassionally others usually being Dahlias, Quercus species and Solidago.

Also sustains: Water Ermine Spilosoma urticae / papyratia, Archer's Dart Agrotis vestigialis / valligera, Feathered

Ranunculus Eumichtis lichenea, Sweet-Gale Apatele euphorbiae / myricae, Frosted Orange Gortyna flavago /ochracea (in stems), Cinnabar Callimorpha / Euchelta jacobaea, Gem moth Nycterosea obstipata / fluviata / gemmata, Lime-speck Pug Eupithecia centaureata / oblongata (eats flowers), Wormwood Pug Eupithecia absinthiata / minutata, Common Pug Eupithecia vulgata, Tawny-speckled Pug Eupithecia icterata / subfulvata, Wood Tiger Nemeophila / Parasemia plantaginis, and Garden Tiger Arctia caia.

Flowerheads sustain another Lepidoptera caterpillar Homoeosoma nebulella which although eating the plant will also eat any gall fly larvae there as well.

Senecio sylvaticus, HEATH GROUNDSEL

Plus S. aquaticus, MARSH RAGWORT, and S. erucifolius, HOARY RAGWORT

Sustain the pretty Cinnabar moth Callimorpha / Euchelta jacobaea.

Senecio viscosus, STINKING GROUNDSEL

Sustains Bordered Straw Heliothis peltigera (mostly eats flowers and seeds).

Senecio vulgaris, GROUNDSEL

Sustains 23 Lepidoptera larva: Wood Tiger Parasemia plantaginis, Scarlet Tiger Panaxia dominula, Dotted Rustic Rhyacia simulans / pyrophila, Flame Shoulder Ochropleura plecta, Setaceous Hebrew Character Amathes e-nigrum, Red Chestnut Cerastis rubricosa, Pale-shouldered Brocade Hadena thalassina, Deep Brown Dart Aporophyla lutulenta, Feathered Ranunculus Eumichtis lichenea, Small Mottled Willow Laphygma exigua, Vine's Rustic Caradrina ambigua, Gold Spangle Plusia bractea, Plain Golden Y Plusia iota, Beautiful Golden Y Plusia pulchrina, Large Twin-spot Carpet Xanthorhoe quadrifasiata, Red Carpet moth Xanthorhoe munitata, Dark-barred Twin-spot Carpet Xanthorhoe ferrugata / unidentaria, Red Twin-spot Carpet Xanthorhoe spadicearia / ferrugata, Gem moth Nycterosea obstipata / fluviata / gemmata, Lime-speck Pug Eupithecia centaureata / oblongata (flowers), Wormwood Pug Eupithecia absinthiata / minutata, and Cinnabar Callimorpha jacobaea

Suffers Scarce Bordered Straw Heliothis armigera.

Serratula tinctoria, SAWWORT,

One of two sustainers Reddish Buff Acosmetia caliginosa other being Poterium sanguisorba.

Also sustains Mouse Amphipyra tragopogonis.

Silene acaulis, MOSS CAMPION

Sustains: Lychnis Hadena bicruris / capsincola, Tawny Shears Hadena lepid / carpophaga (unripe seeds), Campion Hadena cucubali (leaves and unripe seeds), and Netted Pug Eupithecia venosata / insigniata (in seed capsules).

Silene cucubalus / inflata, BLADDER CAMPION

Sustains 13 Lepidoptera larva.

One of two sustainers The Grey Hadena caesia(in roots) other being S. maritima.

One of three sustainers Sandy Carpet Perizoma flavofasciata / decolorata (flowers and seeds) others being Lychnis species.

Also sustains: Brown-Spot Pinion Anchocelis litura, Dark Brocade Eumichtis adusta, Campion Hadena cucubali (leaves and unripe seeds), Marbled Coronet Hadena conspersa / nana (unripe seeds), Marbled Clover Heliothis dipsacea / viriplaca (flowers and seeds), Lychnis Hadena bicruris / capsincola, Tawny Shears Hadena lepida / carpophaga (unripe seeds), Campion Hadena cucubali (leaves and unripe seeds), Netted Pug Eupithecia venosata / insigniata (in seed capsules), and Common Pug Eupithecia vulgata.

Silene gallica subspecies Anglica, English Catchfly

Sustains: Lychnis Hadena bicruris / capsincola, Tawny Shears Hadena lepida / carpophaga (unripe seeds), Campion Hadena cucubali (leaves and unripe seeds), and Netted Pug Eupithecia venosata / insigniata (in seed capsules).

Silene maritima, Sea Campion

Sustains 12 Lepidoptera larva.

One of two sustainers of 2: The Grey Hadena caesia (roots) other being S. inflata, and Barrett's Marbled Coronet Hadena barrettii / luteago other being Spergularia.

Also sustains: Feathered Brindle Aporophyla australis, Ground Lackey Malacosoma castrensis, Black-Banded Antitype xanthomista / nigrocincta (flowers and seeds), Campion Hadena cucubali (leaves and unripe seeds), Marbled Coronet Hadena conspersa / nana (unripe seeds), Lychnis Hadena bicruris / capsincola, Tawny Shears Hadena lepida / carpophaga (unripe seeds), Campion Hadena cucubali (leaves and unripe seeds), and Netted Pug Eupithecia venosata / insigniata (in seed capsules).

SILENE NOCTIFLORA, NIGHT-FLOWERING CATCHFLY

Sustains: Lychnis Hadena bicruris / capsincola, Tawny Shears Hadena lepida / carpophaga (unripe seeds), and Campion Hadena cucubali (leaves and unripe seeds).

SILENE NUTANS, NOTTINGHAM CATCHFLY

Evening scented flowers open over three nights to attract moths which then lay eggs and caterpillars eat foliage and seeds, but not all, benfitting plant.

Sole sustainer of White Spot Hadena albimacula.

Also sustains: Marbled Coronet Hadena conspersa / nana (unripe seeds), Lychnis Hadena bicruris / capsincola, Tawny Shears Hadena lepida / carpophaga (unripe seeds), Campion Hadena cucubali (leaves and unripe seeds), and Netted Pug Eupithecia venosata / insigniata (in seed capsules).

SILENE OTITES, SPANISH CATCHFLY

Sole sustainer of Viper's Bugloss Anepia irregularis / echii (unripe seeds).

Also sustains: Marbled Clover Heliothis dipsacea / viriplaca (flowers and seeds), and Yellow Belle Aspitates chrearia / citraria.

SINAPSIS ALBA, WHITE MUSTARD

Sustains / suffers: Diamond-back moth Plutella maculipenis, Green-veined White Pieris napi, Bath White Pontia daplidice, and Orange-Tip Anthocaris cardamines.

Sᴉsʏᴍʙʀɪᴜᴍ ᴏꜰꜰɪᴄɪɴᴀʟᴇ, HEDGE MUSTARD

Sustains / suffers: Small White Pieris rapae, Green-veined White Pieris napi, Orange-Tip Anthocaris cardamines, Bath White Pontia daplidice, and Garden Carpet Xanthorhoe fluctuata.

Sᴉsʏᴍʙʀɪᴜᴍ sᴏᴘʜɪᴀ, FLIXWEED

One of two sustainers Grey Carpet Lithostege griseata / nivearia (seed pods) other being Erysium.

One of three sustainers White Colon Heliophobus albicolon (flowers) others being Convolvulus soldanella and Ononis arvensis.

Also sustains: Bath White Pontia daplidice, and Cinnabar Callimorpha jacobaea.

Sᴏʟᴀɴᴜᴍ ᴅᴜʟᴄᴀᴍᴀʀᴀ, WOODY NIGHTSHADE / BITTERSWEET

Sustains Death's-head Hawkmoth Acherontia atropos.

Sᴏʟᴀɴᴜᴍ ᴛᴜʙᴇʀᴏsᴜᴍ, POTATOES

Sustains Death's-head Hawkmoth Acherontia atropos.

Suffers serious damage to roots from Small / Garden Swift Moth Hepialus lupulinus, this also attacks beans, parsnip, lettuce, celery, strawberry and grass roots.

Sᴏʟɪᴅᴀɢᴏ ᴠɪʀɢᴀᴜʀᴇᴀ, GOLDENROD

Flowers rich in nectar.

Sustains 13 Lepidoptera larva.

Sole sustainer of 2: Cudweed Cucullia gnaphalii, and Bleached Pug Eupithecia expallidata (flowers).

One of three sustainers: Starwort Cucullia asteris (flowers) others being Aster and Callistephus.

One of three sustainers Golden Rod Pug Eupithecia virgaureata (flowers) occassionally others usually being Dahlias, Quercus species and Senecio jacobea.

Also sustains: Ruby Tiger Phragmatobia fuliginosa, Ashworth's Rustic Amathes ashworthii, Beautiful Brocade Hadena contigua, Sussex Emerald Thalera fimbrialis, Satin Wave Sterrha subsericeata, Wormwood Pug Eupithecia absinthiata / minutata, Common Pug Eupithecia vulgata, Lime-speck Pug Eupithecia centaureata / oblongata (flowers), and V Pug Chloroclystis coronata (flowers).

Suffer Cephasia species Tortrix moths.

SONCHUS ARVENSIS, PERENNIAL / FIELD MILK / CORN SOW-THISTLE

Sustains: Striped Hawkmoth Celerio livornica, Shark Cucullia umbratica, and Broad-barred White Hadena serena (flowers and seeds).

SONCHUS OLERACEUS, SMOOTH / COMMON SOW-THISTLE

Sustains: Shark Cucullia umbratica, and Broad-barred White Hadena serena (flowers and seeds).

SONCHUS PALUSTRIS, MARSH SOW-THISTLE

Sustains Shark Cucullia umbratica.

Sorbus aria, WHITEBEAM

Sustains: Brimstone Moth Opisthographtis luteolata / crataegata, and occasionally Large Tortoiseshell Nymphalis polychloros.

Sorbus aucuparia, ROWAN / MOUNTAIN ASH

Sustains 13 Lepidoptera larva.

One of two sustainers Welsh Wave Venusia cambrica other being Betula.

One of three sustainers Small Yellow Wave Hydrelia flammeolaria / luteata others being Acer campestre and Alnus.

Also sustains: Oak Eggar Lasiocampa quercus, Privet Hawkmoth Sphinx ligustri, Coxcomb Prominent Lophopteryx capucina / camelina, Chinese Character Cilix glaucata / spinula, Chevron Lygris testate (in Hebrides), Mottled Pug Eupithecia exiguata, Brimstone Moth Opisthographtis luteolata / crataegata, suffers Buff-Tip Phalera bucephala, Emperor Saturnia pavonia / carpini Double-striped Pug Gymnoscelis pumilata (flowers), and Yellow-barred Brindle Acasis viretata (flowers first, then green berries then leaves).

Sorbus torminalis, SERVICE TREE

Sustains Brimstone Moth Opisthographtis luteolata / crataegata.

Sparganium erectum, BRANCHED BUR-REED

One of three sustainers of 2: Reed Tussock Laelia caenosa others being Cladium and Phragmites australis, and Bulrush Wainscot Nonagria typhae / arundinis (in stem) others being Typha species.

Also sustains: Reed Wainscot Nonagria algae / cannae (in stem), Webb's Wainscot Nonagria sparganii (in leaf stem), and Gold Spot Plusia festucae.

SPARGANIUM SIMPLEX, SIMPLE BUR-REED
Sustains Gold Spot Plusia festucae.

SPARTIUM JUNCEUM, SPANISH BROOM
Sustains Long Tailed Blue Lampides boeticus (flowers and seeds).

SPERGULA ARVENSIS, SPURRY
Sustains White-line Dart Euoxa tritici / aquilina.

SPERGULARIA RUBRA, RED SPURREY / PURPLE SANDWORT
Sustains Bordered Straw Heliothis peltigera (mostly eats flowers and seeds).

SPERGULARIA RUPICOLA /MARGINATA, SAND-SPURREY / SEA SPURREY
Sole sustainer of Fulvous Clover Heliothis maritime / septentrionalis.

One of two sustainers Barrett's Marbled Coronet Hadena barrettii / luteago (on roots) other being Silene maritima.

Stachys arvensis, FIELD WOUNDWORT

Flowers rich in nectar.

Sustains: Rosy Rustic Hydraecia micacea, and Sub-angled Wave Scopula nigropunctata / strigilaria.

Stachys officinalis / Betonica officinalis, WOOD BETONY

Sustains: Speckled Yellow Pseudopanthera macularia, and possibly Portland Ribbon Wave Sterrha degeneraria.

Stachys sylvatica, HEDGE / WOOD WOUNDWORT

One of two sustainers Small Rivulet Perizoma alchemillata / rivulata (seeds) other being Galeopsis.

Also sustains: Plain Golden Y Plusia iota, Sub-angled Wave Scopula nigropunctata / strigilaria, and Speckled Yellow Pseudopanthera macularia.

Stellaria media, CHICKWEED

see also Cerastium species.

Sustains over 50 Lepidoptera larva.

One of two sustainers of 2: Barred Carpet Perizoma taeniata other being mosses, and Marsh Pug Eupithecia palustraria / pygmaeata (flowers) other being Cerastium.

One of three sustainers of 3: Small Square-spot Diarsia rubi / bella others being Rumex species and Taraxacum, Rustic Caradrina blanda / taraxaci others being Plantago and Rumex species, and Sharp-angled Carpet Euphyia unangulata others being Alsine and Rubus idaeus.

Also sustains: Muslin Cycnia mendica, Clouded Buff Diacrisia sannio / russula, Archer's Dart Agrotis vestigialis / valligera, Heart and Dart Agrotis exclamationis, Portland Moth Actebia praecox, Northern Rustic Ammogrotis lucernea, Flame Shoulder Ochropleura plecta, Autumnal Rustic Amathes glareosa, Dotted Clay Amathes baia, Setaceous Hebrew Character Amathes e-nigrum, Triple-spotted Clay Amathes ditrapezium, Double Square-spot Amathes triangulum, Square-spotted Clay Amathes stigmatica / rhomboides, Square-spot Rustic Amathes xanthographa, Lesser Yellow Underwing Triphaena comes / orbona, Lunar Yellow Underwing Triphaena orbona / subsequa, Lesser Broad-border Triphaena lanthina,White-marked Gypsitea leucographa, Red Chestnut Cerastis rubricosa, Shears Hada nana / dentina, Light Brocade Hadena w-latinum / genistae, Clay Leucania lithargyria, Deep Brown Dart Aporophyla lutulenta, Black Rustic Aporophyla nigra, Feathered Brindle Aporophyla australis, Feathered Ranunculus Eumichtis lichenea, Beaded Chestnut Agrochola lychnidis / pistacina, Clouded Brindle Apamea characterea / hepatica / tincta, Mottled Rustic Caradrina morpheus, Uncertain Caradrina alsines, Vine's Rustic Caradrina ambigua, Pale Mottled Yellow Caradrina clavipalpis / cubicularis / quadripunctata, Satin Wave Sterrha subsericeata, Bright Wave Sterrha ochrata / ochrearia, Plain Wave Sterrha inornata, Riband Wave Sterrha aversata, Blood-vein Calothysanis amata / amataria, Large Twin-spot Carpet Xanthorhoe quadrifasiata, Red Carpet moth Xanthorhoe munitata, Dark-barred Twin-spot Carpet Xanthorhoe ferrugata / unidentaria, Red Twin-spot Carpet Xanthorhoe spadicearia / ferrugata, Twin-spot Carpet Colostygia didymata, and Yellow Shell Euphyia bilineata.

STELLARIA AQUATICA, WATER STITCHWORT

Plus S. holostea GREATER STITCHWORT, S. graminea LESSER STITCHWORT and S. media are

<u>One of two sustainers</u> Cloaked Carpet Euphyia picata other being Cerastium species.

STEREUM HIRSUTUM, YELLOW-RIBBED BRACKET FUNGUS

Sustains Waved Black Parascotia fuliginaria.

SUEDA MARITIME, SEA BLITE

Sustains Sand Dart Agrotis ripae.

SYMPHORICARPUS RACEMOSA, SNOWBERRY

Sustains 6 Lepidoptera larva.

<u>One of two sustainers</u> Broad-bordered Bee-Hawkmoth Hemaris fuciformis / bombyliformis other being Lonicera.

Also sustains: Marsh Greasy Fritillary Euphydryas aurinia / artemis, Death's-head Hawkmoth Acherontia atropos, Mottled Pug Eupithecia exiguata, Lilac Beauty Apeira syringaria, and occasionally Privet Hawkmoth Sphinx ligustri.

SYMPHYTUM ASPERUM / OFFICINALE, COMFREY

Flowers are rich in nectar.

Sustains Scarlet Tiger Panaxia dominula.

Syringa vulgaris, LILAC

Sustains 7 Lepidoptera larva.

One of three sustainers Waved Umber Hemerophila abruptaria others being Ligustrum and Ribes species.

Also sustains: Privet Hawkmoth Sphinx ligustri, Hebrew Character Orthosia gothica, Pale Pinion Lithophane socia / petrificata, Grey Chi moth Antitype chi, August Thorn ennomos quercinaria / angularia, and Lilac Beauty Apeira syringaria.

TAMARIX GALLICA / PENTANDRA, TAMARISK

<u>Sole sustainer of</u> Tamarisk Pug Eupithecia innotata ssp. tamarisciata.

Also sustains Brown Brocade / Bright-line Brown Eye Diataraxia oleracea.

TANACETUM / CHRYSANTHEMUM VULGARE, TANSY

Flowers are rich in nectar and are visited by at least 27 different insect species: 5 species butterflies and moths, 7 species bee, 7 species flies and 8 other.

Sustains: Wormwood Pug Eupithecia absinthiata / minutata, Tawny-speckled Pug Eupithecia icterata / subfulvata (eats flowers), and Bordered Pug Eupithecia succenturiata.

TARAXACUM OFFICINALE, DANDELION

Blooms open 7am and close 5pm and during rain, unpleasantly scented these blooms are rich in nectar and pollen, attract at least 93 different insect species: 7 species butterflies and moths, 58 species bees, 21 species flies and 7 other.

Sustains 26 Lepidoptera larva.

<u>One of two sustainers</u> Small Fan-footed Wave Sterrha biselata / bisetata (on withered leaves) other being Polygonum aviculare.

<u>One of three sustainers of 6</u>: Light Feathered Rustic Agrotis cinerea others being Rumex species and Thymus, Shuttle-Shaped Dart Agrotis puta / radius others being Polygonum arvense and

Rumex species, Stout Dart Spaelotis ravida / obscura others being Leontodon and Rumex species, Red-headed Chestnut Conistra erythrocephala feeds on Quercus species first then on Taraxacum if underneath), Small Square-spot Diarsia rubi / bella others being Rumex species and Stellaria, and Dwarf Cream Wave Sterrha fuscovenosa / interjectaria / dilutaria / osseata others being Anagallis and Polygonum arvensis (and possibly mosses overwinter).

Also sustains: Dotted Rustic Rhyacia simulans / pyrophila, Clouded Buff Diacrisia sannio / russula, Triple-spotted Clay Amathes ditrapezium, Square-spotted Clay Amathes stigmatica / rhomboides, Great Brocade Eurois occulta, Pale Shining Brown Polia nitens / advena, Shears Hada nana / dentina, Clay Leucania lithargyria, Feathered Ranunculus Eumichtis lichenea, Small Mottled Willow Laphygma exigua, Mottled Rustic Caradrina morpheus, Vine's Rustic Caradrina ambigua, Common Emerald Hemithea aestivaria / strigata / thymiaria (before hibernation), Isle of Wight Wave Sterrha humiliata / osseata, Satin Wave Sterrha subsericeata, Flame Carpet Xanthorhoe designata / propugnata, Plain Wave Sterrha inornata, Riband Wave Sterrha aversata, Yellow Shell Euphyia bilineata, and Belted Beauty Nyssia zonaria.

TAXUS BACCATA, YEW
Sustains Satin Beauty moth Deileptenia ribeata / abietaria.

TEUCRIUM SCORODONIA, WOOD SAGE
Flowers are rich in nectar.

Sustains: Heath Fritillary Melitaea athalia, Mullein Wave Scopula marginepunctata / promutata / incanata, Twin-spot Carpet Colostygia didymata, and Speckled Yellow Pseudopanthera macularia.

THALICTRUM AQUILEGIFOLIUM, GREATER MEADOW-RUE

One of two sustainers Purple-shaded Gem Plusia variabilis / illustris other being Aconitum.

THALICTRUM FLAVUM, YELLOW MEADOW-RUE

One of two sustainers Marsh Carpet Perizoma sagittata (unripe seeds) other T. minus.

THALICTRUM MINUS, LESSER MEADOW-RUE

One of two sustainers Marsh Carpet Perizoma sagittata (unripe seeds) other T. flavum.

THLASPI ARVENSE, FIELD PENNYCRESS

Sustains Bath White Pontia daplidice.

THYMUS SPP. THYMES

Sustains 12 Lepidoptera.

Sole sustainer of 2: Thyme Pug Eupithecia distinctaria / constrictata (flowers and seeds), and Large Blue Maculinea arion- which interestingly after their last moult may eat the larvae of Myrmica scabrinodis or M. laevinodis ants.

One of two sustainers of 2: Lace Border Scopula ornata / paludata other being Oreganum, and Pinion-streaked Snout Schranckia costaestrigalis other being Mentha.

One of three sustainers Light Feathered Rustic Agrotis cinerea others being Rumex species and Taraxacum.

Also sustains: Dotted-Border Wave Sterrha sylvestraria / straminata, Ashworth's Rustic Amathes ashworthii, Sussex Emerald Thalera fimbrialis, Lewes Wave Scopula immorata, Annulet Gnophos obscurata / pullata, Straw Belle Aspitates gilvaria, and V Pug Chloroclystis coronata (flowers).

Tilia cordata SMALL-LEAVED LIME
Sole sustainer of Scarce Hook-Tip Drepana harpagula sicula.

Tilia europaea, LIMES
Sustain 24 Lepidoptera.

Sole sustainer of 2: Orange Sallow Tiliacea citrago, and December Moth Poecilo campapopuli.

Also sustains: Lime Hawkmoth Mimas tiliae, Lobster Moth Stauropus fagi and Coxcomb Prominent Lophopteryx capucina / camelina, Black V moth Leucoma v-nigrum / l-album, Sprawler Brachyonycha sphinx / cassinia. Grey Dagger Apatele psi, Lunar-Spotted Pinion Cosmia pyralina, Common Emerald Hemithea aestivaria / strigata / thymiaria (after hibernation), Broken-barred Carpet Electrophaeus corylata, Red-green Carpet Chloroclysta siterata / psittacata, August Thorn Ennomos quercinaria / angularia, Canary-shouldered Thorn Deuteronomos alniaria / tiliaria, September Thorn, Deuteronomos erosaria, Scarce Umber Eriannis aurantiara, suffers Buff-Tip Phalera bucephala, Gipsy Moth Lymantria dispar, Black Arches Lymantria monacha, Hebrew Character Orthosia gothica, Pale Pinion Lithophane socia / petrificata, Swordgrass Xylena exsoleta, and Olive Crescent Trisateles emortualis (dead leaves and lichens).

TRIFOLIUMS, CLOVERS & TREFOILS
Sustain 8 Lepidoptera larva on most species.

Interestingly Burnet moth caterpillars seek Birdsfoot trefoil plants with higher cyanide levels as this then protects them.

<u>One of three sustainers</u> Bordered Grey Selidosema plumaria / ericetaria others being Calluna vulgaris and Sarothamnus.

Also sustains: Belted Beauty Nyssia zonaria, Lesser Yellow Underwing Triphaena comes / orbona, Hebrew Character Orthosia gothica, Beaded Chestnut Agrochola lychnidis / pistacina, Common Emerald Hemithea aestivaria / strigata / thymiaria (before hibernation), and Black-veined Moth Siona lineata / dealbata.

TRIFOLIUM CAMPESTRE, HOP-TREFOIL
and T. dubium, LESSER YELLOW TREFOIL

Sustain in addition to 8 Lepidoptera larva found on most species: Scarce Black Arches Celama aerugula / centonalis (flowers and leaves), and Bordered Straw Heliothis peltigera (mostly eats flowers and seeds).

Trifolium dubium, LESSER YELLOW TREFOIL

Sustains in addition to 8 Lepidoptera larva found on most species: Silver Cloud Xylomiges conspicullaris, and Bordered Straw Heliothis peltigera (mostly eats flowers and seeds).

Trifolium pratense, RED / PURPLE CLOVER

Once known as Bee Bread

Flowers are particularly rich in nectar.

Sustains 13 Lepidoptera larva in addition to 8 Lepidoptera larva found on most species: Grass Eggar Lasiocampa trifolii, Pearly Underwing Peridroma porphyrea / saucia, Common Blue Polyommatus icarus / alexis, Mazarine Blue Cyaniris semiargus / acis, Pale Clouded Yellow Colias hyale, Clouded Yellow Colias croceus / edusa, Mother Shipton Euclidimera mi, Burnet Companion Eetypa glyphica, Scarce Black Arches Celama aerugula / centonalis (flowers and leaves), Marbled Clover Heliothis dipsacea / viriplaca (flowers and seeds), Chalk Carpet Ortholitha bipunctaria, and Bloxworth Blue Everes argiades / tiresias (flowers and leaves).

Suffers Garden Dart Euoxa nigricans.

Trifolium repens, WHITE / DUTCH CLOVER

Sustains 14 Lepidoptera in addition to 8 Lepidoptera larva found on most species: Heart & Club Agrotis clavis / corticea, Common Blue Polyommatus icarus / alexis, Mazarine Blue Cyaniris semiargus / acis, Pale Clouded Yellow Colias hyale, Clouded Yellow Colias croceus / edusa, Mother Shipton Euclidimera mi, Burnet Companion Eetypa glyphica, Shaded Broad-Bar Ortholitha chenopodiata / limitata / mensuraria, Chalk Carpet Ortholitha bipunctaria, Latticed Heath Chiasma clathrata, Scarce Black Arches Celama aerugula / centonalis (flowers and leaves),

Bloxworth Blue Everes argiades / tiresias (flowers and leaves), and Hoary Footman Eilema caniola (algae and lichens).

Suffers Garden Dart Euoxa nigricans.

TRIPLEUROSPERMUM INODORUM / MATRICARIA INODORA, SCENTLESS MAYWEED

Sustains: Lesser Broad-border Triphaena lanthina, and Bordered Straw Heliothis peltigera (mostly eats flowers and seeds).

TRITICUM AESTIVUM / TURGIDUM / VULGARE, WHEAT / CORN

Sustains 6 Lepidoptera larva.

Sole sustainer of Rustic Shoulder-Knot Apamea sordens / basilinea (seeds, possibly of other grasses).

One of three sustainers Flounced Rustic Luperina testacea (roots) others being Avena and Hordeum.

Also sustains: Rosy Minor Procus literosa (in stems), Pale Mottled Yellow Caradrina clavipalpis / cubicularis / quadripunctata (seeds), Rosy Rustic Hydraecia micacea (in stems), and Brighton Wainscot Oria musculosa (in stem).

TROLLIUS EUROPAEUS, GLOBE-FLOWER

Sustains Golden Plusia Polychrisia moneta (on seed pod first).

Tropaeolum majus, NASTURTIUMS

Suffer Large White Pieris brassicae.

Tussilago farfara, COLTSFOOT

Flowers are rich in nectar.

Sustains: Cinnabar Callimorpha jacobaea, Glaucous Shears Hadena bombycina / glauca, and Belted Beauty Nyssia zonaria.

Typha angustifolia, LESSER REED-MACE

One of two sustainers Bulrush Wainscot Nonagria typhae / arundinis (in stems) others being Sparganium and **T.** latifolia.

Also sustains: Reed Wainscot Nonagria algae / cannae (in stems), and Webb's Wainscot Nonagria sparganii (in stems).

Typha latifolia, GREAT REED-MACE

One of three sustainers Bulrush Wainscot Nonagria typhae / arundinis (in stem) others being Sparganium and **T.** angustifolia.

Also sustains: Reed Wainscot Nonagria algae / cannae (in stems), and Webb's Wainscot Nonagria sparganii (in stems).

— U —

ULEX EUROPAEUS, FURZE / GORSE

Especially useful as seldom out of flower.

Sustains 17 Lepidoptera larva.

<u>Sole sustainer of</u> Scottish Belle Ortholitha scotica.

One of three sustainers Grass Emerald Pseudoterpna pruinata / cytisaria others being Genista and Sarothamnus.

Also sustains: Grass Eggar Lasiocampa trifolii, Grass Wave Perconia strigillaria, Mazarine Blue Cyaniris semiargus / acis, Dark Tussock Dasychira fascelina. Silver-Studded Blue Phlebius argus / aegon, Beautiful Brocade Hadena contigua, Bordered Straw Heliothis peltigera, Small Grass Emerald Chlorissa viridata, Lead Belle Ortholitha mucronata / plumbaria / palumbaria, Green Hairstreak Callophrys rubi (flowers and leaves), Long Tailed Blue Lampides boeticus (flowers and seeds), Bloxworth Blue Everes argiades / tiresias (flowers and leaves), Holly / Azure Blue Celastrina argiolus (flowers, flower buds, green berries and leaves), and Double-striped Pug Gymnoscelis pumilata (flowers).

Suffers Cream-spot Tiger Arctia villica.

ULMUS CAMPESTRIS / PROCERA, COMMON / ENGLISH ELM

Sustains 39 Lepidoptera larva.

<u>Sole sustainer of 3</u>: Lesser Spotted Pinion Cosmia affinis, White Spotted Pinion Cosmia diffinis, and Least Carpet Sterrha rusticata.

One of two sustainers of 2: Alchemist Catephia alchymista other being Quercus species, and Dusky-Lemon Sallow Cirrhia gilvago (seeds) other being other Ulmus species.

One of three sustainers of 3: Chestnut Conistra vaccinii others being other Ulmus and Quercus species, Clouded Magpie Abraxas sylvata / ulmata others being Corylus species and Betula, and White Letter Hairstreak Strymonidia w-album others being other Ulmus species and Fraxinus.

Also sustains: Camberwell Beauty Nymphalis antiopa, Lime Hawkmoth Mimas tiliae, December Moth Poecilo campapopuli, Lesser Broad-border Triphaena lanthina (after hibernation), Brown Brocade / Bright-line Brown Eye Diataraxia oleracea, Common Quaker Orthosia stabilis, Twin-Spotted Quaker Orthosia munda, Clouded Drab Orthosia incerta / instabilis, Sprawler Brachyonycha sphinx / cassinia, Flounced Chestnut Anchocelis helvola / rufina, Copper Underwing Amphipyra pyramidea, Large Tortoiseshell Nymphalis polychloros, Comma Polygonia c-album, Scarce Vapourer Orgyia recens / gonostigma, Satellite Eupsilia transversa / satellitia, Lunar-Spotted Pinion Cosmia pyralina, Brick Agrochola circellaris / ferruginea (flowers and seeds), November Moth Oporinia dilutata / nebulata, Pale November Moth Oporinia christyi, Magpie Abraxas grossulariata, August Thorn Ennomos quercinaria / angularia, Canary-shouldered Thorn Deuteronomos alniaria / tiliaria, Lunar Thorn Selenia lunaria, Scarce Umber Eriannis aurantiara, Small Brindled Beauty Apocheima hispidaria, and Hedge Dagger Acronycta psi.

Suffers: Buff-Tip Phalera bucephala, Gipsy Moth Lymantria dispar, Black Arches Lymantria monacha, Emperor Saturnia pavonia / carpini, and Goat Moth Cossus ligniperda (wood live and dead).

Ulmus glabra, WYCH ELM

Sustains 16 Lepidoptera larva.

Sole sustainer of Blomer's Rivulet Discoloxia blomeri.

One of two sustainers: Dusky-Lemon Sallow Cirrhia gilvago (seeds) other being other Ulmus species.

One of three sustainers of 2: Clouded Magpie Abraxas sylvata / ulmata others being Corylus and Fagus, and White Letter Hairstreak Strymonidia w-album others being other Ulmus species and Fraxinus.

Also sustains: Large Tortoiseshell Nymphalis polychloros, Comma Polygonia c-album, Scarce Vapourer Orgyia recens / gonostigma, Satellite Eupsilia transversa / satellitia, Brick Agrochola circellaris / ferruginea (flowers and seeds), Autumnal Moth Oporinia autumnata, and Pale November Moth Oporinia christyi.

Suffers: Buff-Tip Phalera bucephala, Gipsy Moth Lymantria dispar, Black Arches Lymantria monacha, Emperor Saturnia pavonia / carpini, and Goat Moth Cossus ligniperda (wood live and dead).

Urtica dioica, STINGING NETTLES

Sustains 31 Lepidoptera species recorded as supported as larvae, and 4 as adults, with 9 found almost solely on nettles.

Sole sustainer of 3: Spectacle Abrostola tripartita / urticae / triplasia, Stout Snout Hypena obesalis, and Mother-of-pearl Pleuroptya ruralis.

One of two sustainers of 7: Dark spectacle A. triplasia / trigemina other being Humulus, Snout Hypena proboscidalis other being Humulus, Nettle-tap Anthophila fabriciana other being Parietaria, Peacock Nymphalis / Inachis io other being Humulus, Small Tortoiseshell Aglais urticae other **U**. urens, Bloxworth Snout Hypena obsitalis other being Parietaria, and Cyclamen tortrix Clepsis spectrana other being Rumex species.

One of three sustainers Red Admiral Vanessa atalanta others being Humulus and Parietaria.

Also sustains: Painted Lady Vanessa cardui, Comma Polygonia c-album, Scarlet Tiger Panaxia dominula, Lesser Yellow Underwing Triphaena comes / orbona, Brown Brocade / Bright-line Brown-eye Lacanobia / Diataraxia oleracea, Burnished Brass Diachrysia / Plusia chrysitis, Gold Spangle Plusia bractea, Plain Golden Y Plusia iota, Beautiful Golden Y Plusia pulchrina, Dot Melanchra persicariae, Flame Axylia putris, Udea olivalis & U. prunalis, Small magpie Eurrhypara hortulata, Angle shades Phlogophora meticulosa, and occasionally Small Angle-Shades Euplexia lucipara.

Suffer: Yellow / Gold Tail Euproctis similes / auriflua, and Garden Tiger Arctia caia attacks .

Urtica urens, SMALL NETTLE

One of two sustainers of 2: Small Tortoiseshell Aglais urticae other U. dioica, and Nettle-tap Anthophila fabriciana other U. dioica.

<u>One of three sustainers</u> Red Admiral Vanessa atalanta others being Humulus and Parietaria.

Usnea barbata, BEARD LICHEN

<u>Sole sustainer of 2</u>: Dotted Carpet Alcis jubata / glabraria, and Brussels Lace Cleorodes lichenaria.

VACCINIUM SPECIES

Our native Bilberry, V. myrtillus and Cranberry, V. oxycoccus have recently been superceded in the garden by the more productive American versions of Blueberry, V. corymbosum hybrids and Cranberry, **V.** macrocarpon, these may well soon exhibit similar co-lives as the natives.

VACCINIUM MYRTILLUS, BILBERRY

Flowers richer in nectar than V. uliginosum.

Sustains 46 Lepidoptera larva.

Sole sustainer of 2: Bilberry Pug Chloroclystis debiliata, and Rannoch Looper Itama brunneata / fulvaria / pinetaria.

One of two sustainers of 2: Manchester Treble Bar Carsia paludata / imbutata / sororiata (flowers and leaves) other being V. vitis-idaea, Smoky Wave Scopula ternata / fumata other being Salix repens.

One of three sustainers of 7: Northern Dart Amathes alpicola / hyperborea / alpina others being Arctostaphylos and Empetrum, Cousin German Triphaena sobrina others being Betula and Erica cinerea, Scarce Silver Y Plusia interrogationis others being Calluna vulgaris and V. uliginosum, Beautiful Snout Bomolocha crassalis / fontis others being Erica species, Broad-bordered White Underwing Anarta melanopa others being Arctostaphylos and V. vitis-idaea, Small Autumnal / Carpet Oporinia filigrammaria others being Erica species and Saxafraga aizoides, and Early Moth Theria rupicapraria others being Crataegus and Prunus spinosa.

Also sustains: Green Little Thorn Cepphis advenaria, Hairstreak Callophrys rubi, (blossoms and leaves), Pale Eggar Trichiura crataegii, Fox Moth Macrothylacia rubi, Small Lappet Epicnaptera ilicifolia, Speckled Footman Coscinia cribraria / cribrum (leaves and flowers), Purple Clay Diarsia brunnea, Ingrailed Clay Diarsia festiva / primulae (in spring), Green Arches Anaplectoides prasina / herbida (after hibernation), Great Brocade Eurois occulta (after hibernation), White-marked Gypsitea leucographa, Red Chestnut Cerastis rubricosa, Pale Shining Brown Polia nitens / advena, Hebrew Character Orthosia gothica, Flounced Chestnut Anchocelis helvola / rufina, Light Knotgrass Apatele menyanthidis, Golden-rod Brindle Lithomoia solidaginis, Small Dark Yellow Underwing Anarta cordigera, Scarce Dagger Apatele auricoma, Saxon Hyppa rectilinear, Little Emerald Iodis lactaearia, Plain Wave Sterrha inornata, Clay Triple-lines Cosymbia linearia / trilinearia, Twin-spot Carpet Colostygia didymata, Grey Mountain Carpet Entephria caesiata, Northern Spinach Lygris populata, Common Marbled Carpet Dysstroma truncata / russata/ centumnotata, Dark Marbled Carpet Dysstroma citrata / immanata, July Highflyer Hydriomena furcata / elutata / sordidata, Scallop Shell Calocalpe undulata, Northern Argent & Sable Eulype subhastata, Common Pug Eupithecia vulgata, Autumnal Moth Oporinia autumnata, November Moth Oporinia dilutata / nebulata, and Scalloped Hazel Gonodontis bidentata.

Vaccinium vitis-idaea, COWBERRY / RED WHORTLEBERRY / MOUNTAIN CRANBERRY

Sustains 9 Lepidoptera larva.

One of two sustainers Manchester Treble Bar Carsia paludata / imbutata / sororiata (flowers and leaves) other being V. myrtillus above.

One of three sustainers Broad-bordered White Underwing Anarta melanopa others being Arctostaphylos and V. myrtillus.

Also sustains: Golden-rod Brindle Lithomoia solidaginis, Small Dark Yellow Underwing Anarta cordigera, Saxon Hyppa rectilinear, Grey Mountain Carpet Entephria caesiata, Northern Spinach Lygris populata, November Moth Oporinia dilutata / nebulata, and Green Hairstreak Callophrys rubi (blossoms and leaves).

Vaccinium uliginosum, BOG WHORTLEBERRY

One of three sustainers of 2: Nonconformist Graptolitha lamda others being Salix repens and Myrica gale, and Scarce Silver Y Plusia interrogationis others being Calluna vulgaris and V. myrtillus.

Also sustains: Small Dark Yellow Underwing Anarta cordigera, Northern Argent & Sable Eulype subhastata, and November moth Oporinia dilutata / nebulata.

Valeriana officinalis, VALERIAN

One of two sustainers of 2: Valerian Pug Eupithecia valerianiata (flowers and seeds) other being V. dioica, and Lesser Cream Wave Scopula immutata other being Filipendula.

Also sustains: Mullein Wave Scopula marginepunctata / promutata / incanata, and White Point Leucania albipuncta.

Valeriana dioica, MARSH VALERIAN

One of two sustainers Valerian Pug Eupithecia valerianiata (flowers and seeds) other being V. officinalis.

Also sustains Marsh / Greasy Fritillary Euphydryas aurinia / artemis.

Valerianella spp. CORN SALAD
Sustains Rosy Wave moth Scopula emutaria.

Verbascum, MULLEINS
Flowers supposedly rich in nectar and undoubtedly rich in pollen.

Sustains Satyr Pug Eupithecia satyrata (flowers).

Verbascum nigrum, BLACK MULLEIN
Sustains: Striped Lychnis Cucullia lychnitis, Mullein Shark Cucullia verbasci, and Satyr Pug Eupithecia satyrata (flowers).

Verbascum pulverulentum, HOARY MULLEIN
Sustains: Mullein Shark Cucullia verbasci, and Satyr Pug Eupithecia satyrata (flowers).

Verbascum thapsus, GREAT MULLEIN
Sustains: Cinnabar Callimorpha jacobaea, Setaceous Hebrew Character Amathes e-nigrum, Mullein Shark Cucullia verbasci, and Frosted Orange Gortyna flavago /ochracea (in stems).

Veronica chamaedrys, GERMANDER SPEEDWELL
Sustains: Heath Fritillary Melitaea athalia, Isle of Wight Wave Sterrha humiliata / osseata, Sub-angled Wave Scopula nigropunctata / strigilaria, Straw Belle Aspitates gilvaria, and possibly Portland Ribbon Wave Sterrha degenerari.

Viburnum lantana, WAYFARING-TREE

Sustains Sprawler Brachyonycha sphinx / cassinia.

Viburnum opulus, GUELDER ROSE

Flowers rich with nectar.

Sustains: Common Quaker Orthosia stabilis, and Yellow-barred Brindle Acasis viretata (flowers first, then green berries then leaves).

Viburnum tinus, LAURUSTINUS

Sustains Privet Hawkmoth Sphinx ligustri, as may other V. species.

Vicia, BROAD / FAVA / FIELD BEANS and VETCHES

Sustains: Grass Eggar Lasiocampa trifolii, and Shaded Broad-Bar Ortholitha chenopodiata / limitata / mens uraria.

Vicia cracca, TUFTED VETCH

One of three sustainers Black-neck Lygephila pastinum others being Astragalus glycphyllos and Vicia cracca.

Also sustains: Scarce Black-neck Lygephila craccae, Wood White Leptidea sinapis, and Sub-angled Wave Scopula nigropunctata / strigilaria.

Vicia faba, BEANS, BROAD

Suffer Small / Garden Swift Moth Hepialus lupulinus on roots, also suffers Silver Gamma / Y moth Plusia gamma.

VICIA SEPIUM, BUSH VETCH

Sustains: Scarce Black-neck Lygephila craccae, and Cream Wave Scopula floslactata / remutata / remutaria.

VICIA SYLVATICA, WOOD VETCH

Sustains Scarce Black-neck Lygephila craccae.

VIOLA CANINA, DOG VIOLET

Sustains 13 Lepidoptera larva.

Sole sustainer of High Brown Fritillary Argynnis cydippe / adippe.

Sole sustainers of Dark Green Fritillary Argynnis aglaia are Viola species.

Also sustains: Silver Washed Fritillary Argynnis paphia, Clouded Buff Diacrisia sannio / russula, Queen of Spain Fritillary Argynnis lathonia, Small Pearl-Bordered Fritillary Argynnis selene, Pearl-Bordered Fritillary Argynnis euphrosyne, Ingrailed Clay Diarsia festiva / primulae, Plain Wave Sterrha inornata, Sub-angled Wave Scopula nigropunctata / strigilaria, Large Twin-spot Carpet Xanthorhoe quadrifasiata, and Red-headed Chestnut Conistra erythrocephala (oak first then on Violas if underneath).

Suffer Angle Shades Moth

VIOLA HIRTA, HAIRY VIOLET

Sustain 8 Lepidoptera larva.

Sole sustainers of Dark Green Fritillary Argynnis aglaia are Viola species. Also sustains: Small Pearl-Bordered Fritillary Argynnis selene, Pearl-Bordered Fritillary Argynnis euphrosyne, Ingrailed

Clay Diarsia festiva / primulae, Plain Wave Sterrha inornata, Sub-angled Wave Scopula nigropunctata / strigilaria, Large Twin-spot Carpet Xanthorhoe quadrifasiata, and Red-headed Chestnut Conistra erythrocephala (oak first then on Violas if underneath).

Viola lutea, HEARTSEASE

Sustain 10 Lepidoptera larva.

Sole sustainers of Dark Green Fritillary Argynnis aglaia are Viola species. Also sustains; Small Pearl-Bordered Fritillary Argynnis selene, Queen of Spain Fritillary Argynnis lathonia, Pearl-Bordered Fritillary Argynnis euphrosyne, Ingrailed Clay Diarsia festiva / primulae, Plain Wave Sterrha inornata, Sub-angled Wave Scopula nigropunctata / strigilaria, Large Twin-spot Carpet Xanthorhoe quadrifasiata, and Red-headed Chestnut Conistra erythrocephala (oak first then on Violas if underneath).

Suffer Angle Shades Moth

Viola odorata, SWEET VIOLET

Sustains 10 Lepidoptera larva.

Sole sustainers of Dark Green Fritillary Argynnis aglaia are Viola species. Also sustains: Small Pearl-Bordered Fritillary Argynnis selene, Queen of Spain Fritillary Argynnis lathonia, Pearl-Bordered Fritillary Argynnis euphrosyne, Ingrailed Clay Diarsia festiva / primulae, Plain Wave Sterrha inornata, Sub-angled Wave Scopula nigropunctata / strigilaria, Large Twin-spot Carpet Xanthorhoe quadrifasiata, and Red-headed Chestnut Conistra erythrocephala (oak first then on Violas if underneath).

Suffer Angle Shades Moth.

Vinca major GREATER PERIWINKLE

Sustains Six-striped Rustic Amathes sexstrigata / umbrosa.

Vinca minor, LESSER PERIWINKLE

One of three sustainers Oleander Hawkmoth Daphnis nerii others being Cornus mas and Nerium.

Vitis vinifera, GRAPEVINE

Sustains: Striped Hawkmoth Celerio livornica, Silver Striped Hawkmoth Hippotion celerio, and occasionally Elephant Hawkmoth Deilephila elpenor.

— X —

Xanthoria parietina, ORANGE WALL LICHEN

<u>One of two sustainers</u> Beautiful Hook-tip Laspeyria flexula other being Physcia Star lichen.

— Y —

Yucca spp. ADAM'S NEEDLES

American plant there pollinated by a small white moth, this makes a ball of pollen, deliberately inserts this into a special hollow in the top of the stigma of the next flower and lays eggs in the ovary, the larvae consume some of the resultant seed but seldom all, thus both benefit.

— Z —

Zea mays, CORN / MAIZE / SWEET CORN

Sustains Scarce Bordered Straw Heliothis armigera.

Glossary

English plant common names and their Latin genus.

ABELE Populus

ACRID LETTUCE Lactuca

ADAM'S NEEDLES Yucca

AGRIMONY Agrimonia

ALDER Alnus

ALDER-BUCKTHORN Rhamnus

ALFALFA Medicago

ALGERIAN IRIS Iris

ALPINE CURRANT Ribes

ALPINE LADY'S MANTLE Alchemilla

ALPINE MEADOW-GRASS Poa

ALPINE SAXIFRAGE Saxifragas

ALSIKE CLOVER Trifolium

AMARANTH Amaranthus

AMPHIBIOUS BISTORT Polygonum

ANISE Pimpinella

ANISE HYSSOP Agastache

ANNUAL MEADOW-GRASS Poa

APPLE Malus

APRICOT Prunus

ARCTIC SAXIFRAGE Saxifraga

ASPARAGUS BEAN Vigna

ASTER Callistephus

AUTUMN GENTIAN Gentiana

AUTUMN HAWKBIT Leontodon

BABY BLUE EYES Nemophila

BABY'S BREATH Gypsophila

BAJRA Pennisetum

BALSAM Impatiens

BANEBERRY Actaea

BARNYARD GRASS Echinochloa

BARLEY Hordeum

BASIL Ocimum

BASTARD BALM Melittis

BAY Laurus

BEANS Phaseolus & Vicia

BEARBERRY Arctostaphylos

BEAR'S BREECHES Acanthus

BEAUTY BUSH Kolkwitzia

BEE BALM Monarda

BEECH Fagus

BEET Beta

BEETROOT Beta

BELL HEATHER Erica

BENT GRASS Agrostis

BERGAMOT Monarda

BERMUDA GRASS Cynodon

BERSEEM CLOVER Trifolium

BETONY Betonica / Stachys

BILBERRY Vaccinium

BINDWEED Convolvulus

BIRCH Betula

BIRCH BRACKET FUNGUS Polyporus

BIRD CHERRY Prunus

BIRD'S-FOOT Ornithopus

BIRD'S FOOT TREFOIL Lotus

BIRTHWORT Aristolochia

BITING STONECROP Sedum

BITTERCRESS Cardamine

BITTER SNEEZEWEED Helenium

BITTERSWEET Solanum

BLACK BINDWEED Bilderdykia / Polygonum

BLACK BRYONY Tamus

BLACK GRAM Phaseolus

BLACK HOREHOUND Ballota

BLACK MEDICK Medicago

BLACK MULLEIN Verbascum

BLACK NIGHTSHADE Solanum

BLACKBERRIES Rubus

BLACKTHORN Prunus

BLADDER CAMPION Silene

BLADDER SEDGE Carex

BLADDER SENNA Colutea

BLANKET FLOWER Gaillardia

BLAZING STAR Liatris

BLUEBELL Scilla

BLUEGRASS Poa

BOGBEAN Menyanthes

BOG MYRTLE Myrica

BOX Buxus

BOX ELDER Acer

BRACKEN Pteris

BRAKE Pteris

BRANCHED BUR-REED Sparganium

BRANDY-BOTTLE Nuphar

BRISTLY OX-TONGUE Picris

BROAD BEANS Vicia

BROAD-LEAVED WILLOW-HERB Epilobium

BROME GRASS Brachypodium & Bromus

BROOKLIME Veronica

BROOM Cytisus /Sarothamnus

BROOM-RAPES Orobanche

BROWN BENT-GRASS Agrostis

BROWN BRACKET FUNGUS Polyporus

BROWN-RIBBED BRACKET FUNGUS Paxillus

BUCKBEAN Menyanthes

BUCKTHORN Rhamnus

BUCKWHEAT Fagopyrum

BUGLE Ajuga

BUGLOSS Anchusa

BULLACE Prunus

BULBOUS BUTTERCUP Ranunculus

BULRUSH Scirpus

BURDOCK Arctium

BURNET ROSE Rosa

BURNET-SAXIFRAGE Pimpinella

BURNING BUSH Dictamnus

BURR CHERVIL Chaerophyllum

BUSH-GRASS Calamagrostis

BUSH VETCH Vicia

BUTCHER'S BROOM Ruscus

BUTTERBUR Petasites

BUTTERCUPS Ranunculus

BUTTERFLY BUSH Buddleia

BUTTERWORTS Pinguicula

CABBAGE Brassica

CALIFORNIAN POPPY Eschsolzia

CANARY GRASS, Phalaris

CANOLA Brassica

CAPER SPURGE Euphorbia

CAPE HYACINTH Galtonia

CARAWAY Carum

CARDINAL FLOWER Lobelia

CARDOON Cynara

CARLINE THISTLE Carlina

CARNATION SEDGE Carex

CARROT Daucus

CASTOR Ricinus

CATCHWEED Galium

CATNIP Nepeta

CAT'S-EAR Hypochaeris

CAT'S TAIL GRASS Phleum

CAULIFLOWER Brassica

CEDAR Cedrus

CELERY Apium

CENTAURY Erythraea

CHAMOMILE, CORN Anthemis

CHAMOMILE, GERMAN Matricaria

CHAMOMILE, ROMAN Anthemis

CHAMOMILE, STINKING Anthemis

CHARLOCK Brassica & Sinapsis

CHERRY Prunus

CHERRY LAUREL Prunus

CHERVIL Anthriscus

CHESTNUT, HORSE Aesculus

CHESTNUT, SWEET Castanea

CHICKWEEDS Cerastium & Stellaria

CHICKPEA Cicer

CHICORY Cichorium

CHILEAN GLORY FLOWER Eccremocarpus

CHILEAN POTATO TREE Solanum

CHINA ASTER Callistephus

CHINESE CABBAGE / GREENS Brassica

CHIVES Alliums

CHRISTMAS ROSE Hellebore

CINQUEFOIL Potentilla

CLEAVERS Galium

CLIMBING BITTERSWEET Celastrus

CLOVER Trifoliums

CLUSTER BEANS Cyamopis

CLUSTERED BELLFLOWER Campanula

COCK'S-FOOT GRASS Dactylis

COCKSPUR Panicum

COGONGRASS Imperata

COLLARDS Brassicas

COLTSFOOT Tussilago

COLUMBINE Aquilegia

COMFREY Symphytum

CONEFLOWERS Rudbeckia

CONFLUENT LICHEN Lecidea

CORAL FLOWER Heuchara

CORAL-ROOT Cardamine

CORIANDER Coriandrum

CORN CHAMOMILE Anthemis

CORN COCKLE Agrostemma

CORN GROMWELL Lithospermum

CORN MARIGOLD Chrysanthemum

CORN MINT Mentha

CORN SOW-THISTLE Sonchus

CORNEL Cornus

CORNELIAN CHERRY Cornus

CORNFLOWER Centaurea

CORN SALAD Valerianella

COTTON Gossypium.

COTTON-GRASS Eriophorum

COTTON LAVENDER Santolina

COTTON THISTLE Onopordum

COUCH Agropyron

COURGETTE Cucurbita

COWBANE Cicuta

COWBERRY Vaccinium

COW PARSNIP Heracleum

COWSLIP Primula

COW-WHEAT Melampyrum

CRABGRASS Digitaria

CRACK WILLOW Salix

CRANE'S-BILL Geranium

CREEPING CLUB-RUSH Scirpus

CREEPING CROWFOOT Ranunculus

CREEPING SOFT-GRASS Holcus

CREEPING YELLOW-CRESS Rorippa

CRESS Lepidium

CRESTED DOG'S-TAIL GRASS
Cynosurus

CRIMSON CLOVER Trifolium

CROSS-LEAVED HEATH Erica

CROWBERRY Empetrum

CUBAN SPINACH Claytonia

CUCKOO-FLOWER Cardamine

CUCKOO PINT Arum

CUCUMBER Cucumis

CUDWEED Filago / Gnaphalium

CURLED DOCK Rumex

CURRANTS Ribes

CYPRESS Chaemaecyparis

CYPRESS SPURGE Euphorbia

DAFFODIL Narcissus

DAISIES Bellis

DAISY BUSH Olearia

DAME'S VIOLET Hesperis

DANDELION Taraxacum

DARNEL Lolium

DAYLILY Hemerocallis

DEADLY NIGHTSHADE Atropa

DEAD NETTLE Lamium

DEPTFORD PINK Dianthus

DEVIL'S-BIT SCABIOUS Scabiosa

DEVIL'S CLAW Proboscidea

DEWBERRY Rubus

DILL Antheum

DOCK Rumex

DODDER Cuscuta

DOG LICHEN Peltigera

DOG ROSE Rosa

DOGWOOD Cornus

DOUGLAS FIR Pseudotsuga

DUCKWEED LEMNA

DUKE OF ARGYLL'S TEA PLANT
Lycium

DUSTY MILLER Cineraria

DWALE Atropa

DWARF ELDER Sambucus

DWARF JUNIPER Juniperus

DWARF MALLOW Malva

DYER'S GREENWEED Genista

DYER'S ROCKET Reseda

EARTHNUT Conopodium

EGGPLANT Solanum

ELDERBERRY Sambucus

ELMS Ulnus.

ENCHANTER'S NIGHTSHADE Circaea

ENGLISH CATCHFLY Silene

ESPARSETTE Onobrychis

EUROPEAN SILVER FIR Abies

EVENING PRIMROSE Oenothera

EVERGREEN OAK Quercus

EVERLASTING PEA Lathyrus

EYEBRIGHT Euphrasia

FALSE ACACIA Robinia

FALSE-OAT Arrhenatherum

FALSE VALERIAN Centranthus

FAT HEN Chenopodium

FENNEL Foeniculum

FEN-SEDGE Cladium

FENUGREEK Trigonella

FESCUES Festuca

FEVERFEW Chrysanthemum / Matricaria

FIELD BINDWEED Convolvolus

FIELD BROME-GRASS Bromus

FIELD GENTIAN Gentiana

FIELD MAPLE Acer

FIELD MELILOT Melilotus

FIELD MOUSE-EAR CHICKWEED Cerastium

FIELD FORGET-ME-NOT Myosotis

FIELD SCABIOUS Knautia

FIELD SOUTHERNWOOD Artemesia

FIELD WOOD-RUSH Luzula

FIELD WOUNDWORT Stachys

FIG Ficus

FIGWORT Scrophularia

FIORIN Agrostis

FINE BENT Agrostis

FIRS Abies

FIRETHORN Pyracantha

FLAX Linum

FLEABANE Inula & Erigeron

FLIXWEED Sisymbrium

FLOWERING CURRANT Ribes

FLY AGARIC Agaricus

FOXGLOVE Digitalis

FORGET-ME-NOT Myosotis

FRENCH BEANS Phaseolus

FRENCH MARIGOLD Tagetes

FRENCH WILLOW Salix

FROSTED ORACHE Atriplex

FUMITORY Fumaria

GALINGALE Cyperus

GARLIC Allium

GARLIC MUSTARD Alliaria

GAY FEATHER Liatris

GERANIUM (tender) Pelargonium

GERMAN MILLET Setaria

GIPSYWORT Lycopus

GLADDON IRIS Iris

GLAUCOUS SEDGE Carex

GLOBE ARTICHOKE Cynara

GLOBE-FLOWER Trollius

GLOBE THISTLE Echinops

GOJI Lycium

GOLDENROD Solidago

GOATSBEARDS Tragopogon

GOLDEN RAIN TREE Koelreuteria

GOLDEN SAMPHIRE Inula

GOOSEBERRY Ribes

GOOSEFOOT Chenopodium

GOOSEGRASS Galium

GRAM Cicer

GRAIN SORGHUM Sorghum

GRAPE HYACINTH Muscari

GRAPEVINE Vitis

GREATER PERIWINKLE Vinca

GREAT MULLEIN Verbascum

GREAT WOOD-RUSH Luzula

GREATER BURNET-SAXIFRAGE
Pimpinella

GREATER FLEABANE Inula

GREATER KNAPWEED Centaurea

GREATER MEADOW-RUE Thalictrum

GREATER REED-MACE Typha

GREATER STITCHWORT Stellaria

GREATER WATER PARSNIP Sium

GREEN ALKANET Pentaglottis

GREEN AMARANTH Amaranthus

GREENLEAF Desmodium

GREEN NIGHTSHADE Solanum

GROUND ELDER Aegopodium

GROUND IVY Glechoma

GROUNDNUT Apios

GROUNDSEL Senecio

GUELDER ROSE Viburnum

HAGBERRY Prunus

HAIR- GRASS Aira

HAIRY BIRCH Betula

HAIRY NIGHTSHADE Solanum

HAIRY VETCH Vicia

HAIRY WOOD-RUSH Luzula

HAIRY WILLOW-HERB Epilobium

HAREBELL Campanula

HARE'S-TAIL COTTON-GRASS
Eriophorum

HAWKWEEDS Hieracium

HAWKWEED OX TONGUE Picris

HAWTHORN Crataegus

HAZELS Corylus

HEARTSEASE Viola

HEATHER Erica

HEATH FALSE-BROME GRASS
Brachypodium

HEATH BEDSTRAW Galium

HEDGE BEDSTRAW Galium

HEDGE OR BUR PARSLEY Torilis

HEDGE WOUNDWORT Stachys

HEDGE MUSTARD Sisymbrium

HEATH RUSH Juncus

HELIOTROPE Heliotropium

HELLEBORINES Epipactis

HEMLOCK STORK'S-BILL Erodium

HEMP Cannabis

HEMP AGRIMONY Eupatorium

HEMP-NETTLE Galeopsis

HENBANE Hyoscyamus

HERB ROBERT Geranium

HIMALAYAN BALSAM Impatiens

HOARY MULLEIN Verbascum

HOG'S FENNEL Peucedanum

HOGWEED Heracleum

HOLLY Ilex

HOLLYHOCK Alcea & Althaea

HONEYSUCKLES Lonicera

HOLM OAK Quercus

HONESTY Lunaria

HOP Humulus.

HORSE CHESTNUT Aesculus

HOREHOUND Marrubium

HORNBEAM Carpinus

HORSERADISH Armoracia

HORSESHOE VETCH Hippocrepis

HORSETAIL Equisetum

HOUND'S-TONGUE Cynoglossum

HUNGARIAN GRAZING RYE Lolium

HYSSOP Hyssopus

INDIAN BEAN Catalpa

ITALIAN RYEGRASS Lolium

IVY Hedera

IVY-LEAVED TOADFLAX Cymbalaria

JACOBS LADDER Polemonium

JAPANESE ANGELICA TREE Aralia

JAPANESE KNOTWEED Fallopia / Reynoutria

JAPONICA Chaenomeles

JERUSALEM ARTICHOKE Helianthus

JOHNSON GRASS Sorghum

JOINTED RUSH Juncus

JUDAS TREE Cercis

JUNIPER Juniperus

JUTE Corchorus

KALE Brassica

KEMPTON'S WEED Stevia

KIDNEY VETCH Anthyllis

KIWI Actinidia

KNAPWEED Centaurea

KNOTGRASS Polygonum

KNOTTED FIGWORT Scrophularia

KOHL-RABI Brassicas

LABLAB BEANS Lablab

LADY'S BEDSTRAW Galium

LADY'S-MANTLE Alchemilla

LADY'S SMOCK Cardamine

LAMB'S EARS Stachys

LAMBSQUARTERS Chenopodium

LARKSPUR Delphinium

LAURUSTINUS Viburnum

LAVENDER Lavendula

LEAF BEET Beta

LEAFY SPURGE, Euphorbia

LEOPARDS-BANE Doronicum

LEAST LETTUCE Lactuca

LEEKS Allium

LEMON Citrus

LEMON BALM Melissa

LENT ROSE Hellebore

LENTIL Lens

LESSER MEADOW-RUE Thalictrum

LESSER QUAKING-GRASS Briza

LESSER REED-MACE Typha

LESSER SCABIOUS Scabiosa

LESSER STITCHWORT Stellaria

LESSER YELLOW TREFOIL Trifolium

LETTUCE Lactuca

LILAC Syringa

LILY OF THE VALLEY Convallaria

LIME Tillia.

LIMPOGRASS Hemarthria

LING Calluna

LITTLE MOUSE-EAR CHICKWEED Cerastium

LOCUST Robinia

LOOSESTRIFE Lythrum

LORDS AND LADIES Arum

LOTUS Lotus

LOUSEWORT Pedicularis

LOVAGE Levisticum

LOVE IN A MIST Nigella

LUCERNE Medicago

LUNGWORT Pulmonaria

LUPINS Lupinus

LYCHEE TOMATO Solanum

LYME GASS Elymus

MADAGASCAR PRIMROSE Caltharanthus

MADWORT Alyssum

MAIZE Zea

MALE FERN Aspidium

MALLOW Malva

MANY-COLOURED BRACKET FUNGUS Polystictus

MAPLE Acer

MARAM GRASS Psamma

MARJORAM Oreganum.

MARRAM-GRASS Ammophila

MARROW Cucurbita

MARSH BEDSTRAW Galium

MARSH LOUSEWORT Pedicularis

MARSH MARIGOLDS Caltha

MARSH PEA Lathyrus

MARSH SEDGE Carex

MARSH SOW-THISTLE Sonchus

MARSH ST JOHN'S WORT Hypericum

MARSH THISTLE Carduus

MARSH WILLOW-HERB Epilobium

MAT-GRASS Nardus

MAYWEEDS Matricaria & Anthemis

MEADOW BUTTERCUP Ranunuculus

MEADOW CAT'S-TAIL Phleum

MEADOW FESCUE-GRASS Festuca

MEADOW FOX-TAIL Alopecuris

MEADOW GRASSES Poa

MEADOW SAFFRON Colchicum

MEADOW SAXIFRAGE Saxifraga

MEADOW-SWEET Spiraea / Filipendula

MEADOW VETCHLING Lathyrus

MEDLAR Mespilus

MELILOT Melilotus

MELON Cucumis

MEXICAN COCKROACH PLANT Haplophyton

MEZEREON Daphne

MICHAELMAS DAISY Aster

MIGNONETTE Reseda

MILK THISTLE Silybum

MILK-VETCH Astragalus

MILKWEEDS Asclepias

MILKWEED VINE Morrenia

MILKWORT Polygala

MINTS Mentha

MISCANTHUS Miscanthus

MISTLETOE Viscum

MONKSHOOD Aconitum

MORNING GLORY Ipomea

MOSS CAMPION Silene

MOSSY SAXIFRAGE Saxifraga

MOTH BEAN Vigna

MOTHERWORT Leonurus

MOUNTAIN CRANBERRY Vaccinium

MOUNTAIN EVERLASTING Antennaria

MOUNTAIN SAXIFRAGE Saxifraga

MOUSE-EAR CHICKWEED Cerastium

MOUSE-EAR HAWKWEED Hieracium

MUGWORT Artemesia

MULBERRY Morus

MUNG BEAN Vigna

MUSTARD Brassica

NAKED LADIES Colchicum

NARROW-LEAVED RAGWORT Senecio

NASTURTIUMS Tropaeolum

NAVELWORT Cotyledon

NEEDLE-FURZE Genista

NETTLE-LEAVED BELLFLOWER Campanula

NIGHTSHADES Solanum

NOTTINGHAM CATCHFLY Silene

OAKS Quercus

OAT-GRASS Avena / Arrhenatherum

OATS Avena

OKRA Hibiscus/Abelmoschus

OLEANDER Nerium

ONIONS Allium

ORACHE Atriplex

ORANGE Citrus

ORANGE WALL LICHEN Xanthoria

OREGANO Oreganum

OREGON GRAPE Mahonia

ORPINE Sedum

OX EYE DAISY Chrysanthemum

OX TONGUE Picris

PAK CHOI Brassica

PALMER AMARANTH Amaranthus

PANSY Viola

PARSLEY Petroselinum

PARSNIP Pastinaca

PASSION FLOWER Passiflora

PEA Pisum

PEA TREE Caragana

PEACH Prunus

PEAR Pyrus

PEARL MILLET Pennisetum

PELLITORY Parietaria

PENNYCRESS Thlaspi

PENNYROYAL Mentha

PEPPERMINT Mentha

PEPPERS Capsicum

PERPETUAL SPINACH Beta

PERENNIAL RYEGRASS Lolium

PERENNIAL SOW-THISTLE Sonchus

PERFORATED St. JOHN'S WORT Hypericum

PERIWINKLE Vinca

PERUVIAN CHERRY Nicandra.

PETTY SPURGE Euphorbia

PIGEON PEA Cajanus

PIGWEED, Amaranthus retroflexus

PINE Pinus

PINE BRACKET FUNGUS Polystictus

PITCHER PLANT Sarracenia
PLANES Platanus

PLANTAINS Plantago

PLOUGHMANS SPIKENARD Inula

PLUM Prunus

POACHED EGG PLANT Limnanthes

POKEWEED Phytolacca

POPLAR Populus

POPPY Papaver

PORTLAND SPURGE Euphorbia

PORTUGESE LAUREL Prunus

POT MARIGOLD Calendula

POTATOES Solanum

PRICKLY LETTUCE Lactuca

PRICKLY SALTWORT Salsola

PRIMROSE Primula

PRIVET Ligustrum

PROSO MILLET Panicum

PUMPKIN Cucurbita

PURPLE COW-WHEAT Melampyrum

PURPLE NUTSEDGE Cyperus

PURPLE SANDWORT Spergularia

PURPLE SAXIFRAGE Saxifraga

PURPLE SMALL-REED Calamagrostis

PURPLE VIPERS BUGLOSS Echium

PURPLE WILLOW Salix

PURSLANE Portulaca

PYRAMID ORCHID Anacamptis

QUACK GRASS Agropyrum

QUAKING-GRASS Briza

QUICKTHORN Crataegus

QUINCE Chaenomeles / Cydonia

RADISH Raphanus

RAGGED ROBIN Lychnis

RAGWEED Ambrosia / Senecio

RAGWORT Senecio.

RAMSONS Allium

RASPBERRY Rubus.

RAULI Nothofagus

RED BEET Beta

RED BRYONY Bryonia

RED CAMPION Lychnis

RED CLOVER Trifolium

RED DEAD NETTLE Lamium

RED GOOSEFOOT Chenopodium

RED GRASS Digraphis

RED HEMP-NETTLE Galeopsis

RED MILLET Panicum

RED OSIER Cornus

RED RATTLE Pedicularis

REDROOT PIGWEED Amaranthus

REDSHANK Polygonum

RED SPURREY Spergularia

RED WHORTLEBERRY Vaccinium

REED Arundo

REED-GRASS Digraphis

REED MEADOW-GRASS Poa

REFLEXED MEADOW-GRASS Poa

REST-HARROW Ononis

RHUBARB Rheum

RICE Oryza

ROCKET Barbarea

ROCK-ROSE Helianthemum & Cistus

ROSE BAY WILLOWHERB Epilobium

ROSEMARY Rosmarinus

ROSES Rosa

ROUGH BROME-GRASS Bromus

ROUGH CHERVIL Chaerophyllum

ROUND-HEADED RAMPION
Phyteuma

ROWAN Sorbus

RUE Ruta

RUNNER BEANS Phaseolus

RUSH Juncus

RUSSIAN LAVENDER Perovskia

RYE Secale

RYEGRASS Lolium

SAFFLOWER Carthamnus

SAGE Salvia

SAINFOIN Onobrychis

SAINT JOHN'S WORT Hypericum

SAINT PATRICKS CABBAGE Saxifraga

SALAD BURNET Poterium

SALSIFY Tragopogon

SANDBUR Cenchrus

SAND QUITCH Agropyrum

SANDWORT Arenaria / Alsine

SAND-SPURREY Spergularia

SAVORY Satureia

SAWWORT Serratula

SCABIOUS Scabiosa

SCARLET PIMPERNEL Anagallis

SCENTLESS MAYWEED
Tripleurospermum

SEA ASTER Aster

SEA BINDWEED Convolvulus

SEA BLITE Sueda

SEA BUCKTHORN Hippophae

SEA CAMPION Silene

SEA CLUB-RUSH Scirpus

SEA FESCUE-GRASS Festuca

SEA HARD-GRASS Lepturus

SEA HOLLY Eryngium

SEAKALE Crambe

SEA LAVENDER Limonium

SEA MEADOW-GRASS Poa

SEA MILKWORT Glaux

SEA ORACHE Atriplex

SEA ROCKET Cakile

SEA SANDWORT Arenaria

SEA SPURGE Euphorbia

SEA SPURREY Spergularia

SEA WORMWOOD Artemesia

SEDGES Carex

SELF-HEAL Prunella

SERVICE Sorbus

SHALLOTS Allium

SHASTA DAISY Chrysanthemum

SHEEP'S FESCUE Festuca

SHEEP"S SORREL Rumex

SHEPHERD'S PURSE Capsella

SHINING BLACK BRACKET FUNGUS Daldinia

SHINING CRANE'S-BILL Geranium

SHOOFLY Nicandra

SICKLE MEDICK Medicago

SILVERWEED Potentilla

SIMPLE BUR-REED Sparganium

SLENDER FALSE-BROME GRASS Brachypodium

SLENDER St. JOHN'S WORT Hypericum

SLOE Prunus

SMOKE TREE Cotinus

SMOOTH HAWKSBEARD Crepis

SMOOTH MEADOW-GRASS Poa

SMOOTH-PEEL FUNGUS Corticum

SMOOTH SOWTHISTLE Sonchus

SNAKES HEAD FRITILLARY Fritillaria

SNAPDRAGON Antirrhinum

SNEEZEWEED Helenium

SNOWBERRY Symphoricarpus

SNOWDROP Galanthus

SNOWFLAKE Leucojum

SNOWY MESPILUS Amelanchier

SOAPWORT Saponaria

SOLOMONS SEAL Polygonatum

SORGHUM Sorghum

SORREL Rumex

SOUTHERNWOOD Artemesia

SOWBREADS Cyclamen

SOWTHISTLES Sonchus

SOYA Glycine

SPANISH BROOM Spartium

SPANISH CATCHFLY Silene

SPEEDWELL Veronica

SPINACH Spinacia

SPINDLE Euonymous

SPOTTED PERSICARY Polygonum

SPREADING MILLET-GRASS Milium

SPRING SANDWORT Minuartia

SPRUCE Picea

SPURGES Euphorbia

SPURRY Spergula

SQUARE-STEMMED WILLOW-HERB Epilobium

SQUASHES Cucurbita

STAGS HORN SUMACH Rhus

STAR LICHEN Physcia

STARWORT Aster

STATICE Limonium

STRAWBERRY TREE Arbutus

STRAWBERRIES Fragaria

STINGING NETTLE Urtica

STINKING GOOSEFOOT Chenopodium

STINKING GROUNDSEL Senecio

STINKING IRIS Iris

STINKING MAYWEED Anthemis

STINKWEED Diplotaxis

SUCCORY Cichorium

SUGAR BEET Beta

SUGAR MAPLE Acer

SUMMER HYACINTH Galtonia

SUNFLOWER Helianthus

SUN ROSE Cistus

SUN SPURGE Euphorbia

SUPERB LILY Gloriosa

SWAMP BEDSTRAW Galium

SWEDE Brassica

SWEDISH COFFEE Astragalus

SWEET ALYSSUM Alyssum

SWEET CHESTNUT Castanea

SWEET CICELY Myrrhis

SWEET FLAG Acorus

SWEET GALE Myrica

SWEET GUM Liquidamabr

SWEET PEA Lathyrus

SWEET ROCKET Hesperis

SWEET-SCENTED VERNAL GRASS, Anthoxanthum

SWEET TOBACCO Nicotiana

SWEET WILLIAM Dianthus

SWINE CRESS Coronopus

SWISS CHARD Beta

SYCAMORE Acer

SYRIAN SAGE Salvia

TALL FESCUE Festuca

TAMARISK Tamarix

TANSY Tanacetum / Chrysanthemum

TARES Vicia

TARO Colocasia

TARRAGON Artemesia

TEA-LEAVED WILLOW Salix

TEASELS Dipsacus

THISTLES Carduus and Cirsium

THORNAPPLE Datura

THRIFT Armeria

THYME Thymus

TIGER FLOWER Tigridia

TIL Sesamum

TIMOTHY Phleum

TOADFLAX Linaria

TOBACCO Nicotiana

TOMATO Lycopersicon

TOOTHWORT Lathraea

TORMENTIL Potentilla

TOWER MUSTARD Arabis

TRAVELLER'S JOY Clematis

TREACLE MUSTARD Erysimum

TREE MALLOW Lavatera

TREE OF HEAVEN Ailanthus

TREFOIL Trifolium

TUBEROUS PEA Lathyrus

TUFTED DEER'S-GRASS Scirpa

TUFTED HAIR-GRASS Aira

TUFTED SEDGE Carex

TUFTED VETCH Vicia

TULIP TREE Liriodendron

TURNIP Brassica

TWAYBLADE Listera

TWITCH, Agropyrum

UDU Aralia

UNICORN Proboscidea

VALERIAN Valeriana

VIRGINIA CREEPER Parthenocissus

VELVETLEAF Abutilon

VERVAIN Verbena

VETCHES Vicia

VIOLETS Viola

VIPER'S BUGLOSS Echium

VISCID MOUSE-EAR CHICKWEED Cerastium

WALLFLOWERS Cheiranthus

WALL HAWKWEED Hieracium

WALL PENNYWORT Cotyledon (sic)

WALNUTS Juglans

WATER AVENS Geum

WATER BETONY Scrophularia

WATERCRESS Nasturtium

WATER FIGWORT Scrophularia

WATERMELON Citrullus

WATER-MINT Mentha

WATER PLANTAIN Alisma

WATER SPEEDWELL Veronica

WATER STITCHWORT Stellaria

WAYFARING-TREE Viburnum

WEEPING LOVEGRASS Eragrostis

WELD Reseda

WHEAT Triticum

WHITE BEAK-SEDGE Rhynchospora

WHITEBEAM Sorbus

WHITE BRYONY Bryonia

WHITE CAMPION Lychnis

WHITE CHARLOCK Raphanus

WHITE CLOVER Trifolium

WHITE DRYAS Dryas

WHITE MIGNONETTE Reseda

WHITE STONECROP Sedum

WHITE WATERLILY Nymphaea

WHORL FLOWERED CLARY Salvia

WILD BEET Beta

WILD MADDER Rubia

WILD MUSTARD Brassica & Sinapsis

WILD PEA Lathyrus

WILD RADISH Raphanus

WILLOWHERB Epilobium

WILLOW LETTUCE Lactuca

WILLOWS Salix

WINGED SPINDLE Euonymous

WINTER ACONITE Eranthis

WINTERCRESS Barbarea

WINTER HELIOTROPE Petasites

WINTER PURSLANE Claytonia

WITCH Agropyrum

WITCH HAZEL Hamamelis

WOAD Isatis

WOLF'S-BANE Aconitum

WOOD AVENS Geum

WOOD BETONY Stachys

WOODBINE Lonicera

WOODRUFF Asperula

WOOD SORREL Oxalis

WOOD SPURGE Euphorbia

WOOD VETCH Vicia

WOOD WOUNDWORT Stachys

WOODY NIGHTSHADE Solanum

WORMWOOD Artemisia

YARROW Achillea

YELLOW ARCHANGEL Lamiastrum

YELLOW BALSAM Impatiens

YELLOW FIELDRESS Rorippa

YELLOW FIGWORT Scrophularia

YELLOW FLAG Iris

YELLOW FOXTAIL Setaria

YELLOW HORN Xanthocerus

YELLOW LOOSESTRIFE Lysimachia

YELLOW MEADOW-RUE Thalictrum

YELLOW MELILOT Melilotus

YELLOW RATTLE Rhinanthus

YELLOW-RIBBED BRACKET FUNGUS
Stereum

YELLOW ROCKET Barbarea

YELLOW WATERLILY Nuphar

YEW Taxus

YORKSHIRE FOG Holcus

Printed in Great Britain
by Amazon

38948127R00142